M000191634

In reading this book,   *,*
and God's call to excellence in every area of our lives. Bonnie's heart
is to help women recognize their God-given potential and encourage
them to pursue it.

–Lesa A. Ashley
Director of Women's Ministry
Resurrection Life Church
Cadillac, Michigan

Bonnie provides great counsel for every woman who wants to face
life with grace and courage, and be rewarded as a result. As we navi-
gate through life, this book provides guidance on how to stay focused
and live a Godly, satisfying and purposeful life.

–Pastor Duane and Jean E. VanderKlok
Pastors of Resurrection Life Church of Grandville, Michigan
Hosts of a daily national television program, Walking by Faith

Excellence

with

Simple
Elegance

Bonnie Liabenow

Excellence with Simple Elegance
© 2011 Bonnie Liabenow

ALL RIGHTS RESERVED No part of this publication may be reproduced, stored in a retrieval system, or transmitted, in any form or by any means--electronic, mechanical, photocopying, recording, or otherwise--without prior written permission.

Published by Core Communications International
www.coreleaders.net
409 Wedgewood Drive, Cadillac, Michigan 49601

ISBN: 978-0-578-07515-0

Cover design: Bobby Chamberlain, www.bobbyccreative.com
Interior design and typeset: Katherine Lloyd, www.TheDESKonline.com
Editor: Meghan Dryzga, www.copymoves.com

Scripture quotations marked NIV are taken from the *Holy Bible, New International Version*, © 1973, 1978, 1984, International Bible Society. All rights reserved.
Scripture quotations marked KJV are taken from the King James Version of the Bible.
Scripture quotations marked NKJV are taken from the New King James Version, © 1982 by Thomas Nelson, Inc., Publishers.
Scripture quotations marked MSG are taken from *The Message* by Eugene H. Peterson. © 1993, 1994, 1995, 1996, 2000. All rights reserved.
Scripture quotations marked TLB are taken fromThe Living Bible © 1971 by Tyndale House Publishers, Inc. All rights reserved.
Scripture quotations marked CEV are taken fromThe Holy Bible, Contemporary English Version © 1995 by American Bible Society. All rights reserved.
Scripture quotations marked NLT are taken from the Holy Bible, New Living Translation, copyright © 1996, 2004, 2007 by Tyndale House Publishers, Inc.
New Spirit-Filled Life Bible © 2002 by Thomas Nelson, Inc. All rights reserved.

Webster's New Collegiate Dictionary, Merriam-Webster Co, copyright © 1973. All rights reserved.

Printed in the United States by Bethany Press

Table of Contents

ACKNOWLEDGEMENTS

I am especially grateful to Meghan Dryzga, Amber Miller, Katherine Lloyd, Bobby Chamberlain, Andrew MacKay, and Jeff Gerke for their personal commitment and attention to excellence in this project.

My thanks also goes to my family for their encouragement, involvement and support. Thanks for believing in this project.

And to the many pastors for bringing the Word to the church each week that confirmed the writings from my heart; thanks for your obedience to His call on your lives.

FOREWORD

*T*he minute I was put onto Bonnie's book, I knew it was a God thing. Any time an unlikely series of events leads you to discover something you needed in your life (whether you knew it or not) that you otherwise never would have found, you can be sure that's the case. Sometimes the events are understated, other times the series of opportunities are SO unlikely, you wouldn't be surprised to find our Lord and Savior scooping up a helping of shepherd's pie as he settles in at your dinner table. *I thought I heard you come in. We're humbled to say the least. Pass the butter?*

In my case, the latter was closer to the truth. It was during the summer, and I was deeply saturated in my work. I'm a writer, a devoted wife, and a stepmom, but at this time, I was mostly a writer. In addition to my day job as a copywriter, I had made a part-time commitment to edit (read: overhaul) another novel; time was scarce and my family's patience was more-so.

It was a Saturday, and I was submerged in some serious editing when I got a call from my best friend from high school. She explained how she was connected to Bonnie through Bonnie's son. Bonnie had written a book, and my friend wanted me to take a look at it. Do you have time? She asked. *Well, not exactly, as I tip-toed out of ear shot of my husband. What's the premise?* It was a Christian book. *You have my attention.* Not only because I can always use a little more God in my life, but because my best friend is Jewish and very committed to her faith. And yet, she was shopping around a Christian book? Cue the unusual series of events.

Then, in that moment, came the odd and unexpected sensation of the weight of my work's burden being lifted from my shoulders. I had been so anxious and strained about all of these work commitments, and yet, when faced with this request, I wasn't overwhelmed. To the contrary. I might even say I felt… relieved? *That's odd. With this level of excitement and eagerness, you'd think I'd time-traveled to a toast-and-tea breakfast at a harbor-town B&B.*

That's when it hit me: This is important. Coordinated by hands not my own. I'd find time. *Send me the manuscript.*

My intuition (read: God's guidance) was correct. This book was indeed important. It only took me a few pages before I realized it was going to change my perspective, my outlook, my plan and how I operate on a daily basis. This book would help me put my family first, prioritize and organize, pray, love, live patiently, cook, clean, and curl my hair. And I'd do it all on my journey toward excellence.

Like a gust of wind that ushers you into a cozy foyer swelling with fragrant pine and cinnamon, Bonnie's sincere, humble, approachable tones invite you into her thoughts and experiences. And as if in a conversation with a close friend over a warm cup of coffee, she always concedes before she advises. She makes you feel welcome by giving you purpose for being here. She listens to the messages scripture provides us, and shares the experiences of herself and loved ones that His message has helped her through. She shares these experiences gently.

By the end of the first chapter, you'll understand that we all share the same struggles, just in different forms. By the second chapter, you'll understand the power of grounding yourself in faith, family, and community, and you'll answer perhaps the three most important questions of your life. Then, you'll learn how your greatest discomforts can be very rewarding. You'll spend chapter three achieving emotional excellence and chapter four cooking up mental excellence. Then, like the switch of a spotlight on a curtained stage, Bonnie's discussion on the seasons of life helped me understand the importance of recognizing which season I'm actually in, and the value of living in it rather than looking forward to the next one.

Finally, her big reveal: she shows us how do-able a life of excellence is. That it is achieved not through any complicated code or overachieving our womanly duties, but rather in simplicity. A sort of back-to-basics approach at everything from guest towels to pearls. They are the next steps that truly lead us to an uncluttered, purified, more fulfilling life of excellence.

Thanks to Bonnie's words, I need less, and yet I have more. And, much like the way this book landed in my life, that too is a God thing.

–Meghan Dryzga
Senior Copywriter, Author and Editor
December, 2010

Do not let your adornment be merely outward—
arranging the hair, wearing gold, or putting on fine apparel,
rather let it be the hidden person of the heart,
with the incorruptible beauty of a gentle and quiet spirit,
which is very precious in the sight of God.

—1 PETER 3:3–4, NKJV

Introduction
One Woman, Four Parts

Many times we women feel like our lives have no purpose or focus. The demands of life leave us feeling unfulfilled—discontented even. We feel that we're meeting everyone else's needs—our parents', our children's, and our spouse's—but our own needs aren't being met.

A Reference in Life

I clearly recall the eve of my youngest son's high school graduation. Right there, a wave of realization crashed over my soul and mind leaving me discouraged and overwhelmed. I realized that

the last 24 years of my life had been absorbed in my three sons;
like any mother, I had dedicated my life to meeting their needs.
During that time, my identity had gotten lost inside theirs—at
least, in this moment, that's how it seemed. For some crazy reason, I felt they didn't need me.

To heavy the blow, the boys had all chosen lives that didn't
include me anymore—a truth that made it difficult for me to
feel happy about my efforts in getting them to adulthood.

I can't deny that a couple of my sons were living lives that
I wasn't proud of. They had thrown aside the faith I had raised
them with to looser, party-centric lifestyles. One of the boys had
chosen a more disciplined lifestyle, but I still felt that God wasn't
first in his life. All of them were interested in experiencing lifestyles that I had never been in support of.

My impulse thought: Where had I gone wrong? Was my life
so boring that they didn't view me as a good example? All along I
had tried to set a good example for them on how to find purpose
by chasing after God's best, only to feel that it had accomplished
nothing. I became angry at the thought that I had given up a
professional career to stay home to raise these young men, and
this is what I was getting in return. I couldn't understand why
the world was so attractive to them. My life's work appeared to
be crumbling before me in my children's rejection of the lifestyle
they had been accustomed to. I had spent years fulfilling their
needs, but mine were not being met. My purpose and focus was
lost in that moment of turmoil.

It was then that my husband gently reminded me that my work wasn't finished. I would need to step up my prayer life. My boys needed my prayers just as much as they always had, and maybe now more than ever. I chose to hold on to the promise of Proverbs 22:6, "Train up a child in the way he should go, and when he is old he will not depart from it" (NKJV).

What to Expect from this Book: A Simple Plan of Excellence

After several years of extreme concern and pain, I can tell you that by digging my heels into my faith foundation and staying the course, being faithful, loving my children unconditionally and praying like crazy, my sons made a turnaround and are now leading successful lives while understanding the value of leading a God-centered life. Prayer throughout the process of acquiring these tools of excellence led me through turmoil with confidence.

Prayer and practices of this sort are an example of excellence in the Christian life. I call it *excellence with simple elegance*. Learning about the qualities that lead to excellence can shift your thinking and bring about drastic change, not only in your own life but also in the lives of those around you. The pursuit of excellence with simple elegance will bring fulfillment and contentment in your life as a woman of faith, purpose, and focus.

This simple plan of excellence, which is wrapped around biblical principles, will show you how you can experience the abundant life God has planned for you, even when you find yourself in the midst of disappointments and turmoil.

I'll take you through this thought process in a deliberate order.

The Foundation: First, this book will share how to build a foundation for your life with putting God first, family as your number one priority when it comes to human relationships, and community (career/charity work) as your mission field. We will look at the life of a Moabite woman named Ruth from the Old Testament; her story gives great insight into faith, obedience, and commitment that gave her life focus.

Elements of the Heart: Next, we will take a look at the three elements of the heart—prayer, grace, and forgiveness—and how incorporating these elements leads directly to contentment and fulfillment.

Building Blocks: Third, we will take a glance at the life of Queen Esther that her courage, passion, and discipline were the ingredients for a life of excellence, and they were the tools in which she used to save the Jewish nation.

Learning from the Seasons: It is in the seasons (or different stages) of life that these lessons are learned. As women, we make important decisions that set the course of our life and the subsequent seasons to come. You will see how important it is to grab wisdom from each season and how God uses seasons to prepare us for the next. The chapter on seasons will define and give understanding to what they are and how they can lead to contentment.

Physical Excellence: On a separate but similar note, most Christian life-application books for women omit any mention of the physical aspects of life, but I think that's a mistake. Why? Because the physical is where we really live. Therefore this book will discuss the following: routine, organization, and your physical presence including health, figure, clothing, makeup and hair. For most women, how you *look* has a lot to do with how you *feel*. This is not about focusing on the superficial, but rather, your best self in all respects. When a woman doesn't look successful, put together, confident, and beautiful, she most likely won't feel that way either. My simple plan for physical excellence will allow you to pursue life's challenges with confidence.

ONE WOMAN, FOUR PARTS

In your pursuit of a life of excellence with simple elegance, it is necessary to establish yourself in four vital parts of your own life: spiritual, emotional, mental, and physical. You may find this a difficult task or, if you're someone who sees life in black and white, you may find it easier. You may already agree with me on these goals:

Physically, I desire to be healthy and attractive.

Emotionally, I want to be happy, loved, secure, and fulfilled in life.

Mentally, I desire to be a lifetime learner.

Spiritually, my life's focus is to passionately pursue God's call on my life.

With these clear-cut goals, you will see how quickly the right decisions become clear.

GOAL SETTING

The last segment of the book is designed to show you how to begin goal setting. It will be the time to write down your thoughts and prioritize your life. It will be your personal plan of action that will start you on the journey to experience a life of excellence with simple elegance. That chapter will give you the opportunity to commit to excellence in the four aspects of life we just discussed. Ultimately, those are the things that will give your life purpose and focus.

THE RIGHT FRAME OF MIND FOR EXCELLENCE

Proverbs 11:22 tells how undesirable a woman is when she lacks the traits of good taste or discretion. Contrast that against the Proverbs 31 woman, who perceives that her merchandise is of high quality, and we can clearly see the importance of choosing good things. With our goals defined and top-of-mind it is simple to determine if a given opportunity is either very right or very wrong for you. If we are going to be women in pursuit of excellence, we have no choice but to possess good taste, to perceive, evaluate, discern, and delight in good things. Then we'll be like the psalmist in 34:8 "Oh taste and see that the Lord is good." We must choose to run after His goodness.

Once we've made this choice of good taste, it's this conviction that keeps us focused on a clear path to the destiny God has for us. Our convictions keep us from straying away from what is right and good for our life. I think John Osteen (Joel's father) said it best, "If you know God's purpose for your life and focus your energies into fulfilling it, you will run your spiritual race with excellence."

I trust you will find that the pages you hold in hand are so much more than paper and text. They are the result of many years of learning, through trial and error, what it means to be a woman of simple elegance. This book contains practical information and experience I have gained through these lessons, and if you listen close enough, you may just hear my heartbeat.

A Reference in Life:

The Life that Spurred this Approach to Excellence

I have spent my life enjoying family, friends, and playing. As I am a "recreationist" at heart, I have always believed that developing healthy leisure-time activities brings happiness. This led me to acquire a bachelors of science in therapeutic recreation. My mindset has always been to have fun in the sun with the ones I love. And, the bonus is a healthy body. This desire drove me to be disciplined and accomplish my work in a timely fashion. But because I am also a perfectionist, time management sometimes became a challenge. I never wanted to miss a chance to grab my boys and run outside to play. The demands of this life created a natural desire to keep each aspect of my life simple and easy while still maintaining excellence. In this life, I have many lessons, blessings and rewards for my commitment to excellence. For many years my husband and I have been Christmas tree farmers. We still are. In the years of growing Christmas trees, I have learned what hard work is and the discipline that it takes to run a successful business. In raising three successful sons, I know the prayer life that it takes to get them to manhood. My marriage of over 30 years to a wonderful man has allowed me to experience pure joy, passionate love, and undying commitment. As a musician and teacher, God has graciously allowed me to experience real passion.

That's not to say my life has not been without mistakes, sacrifice, pain, disappointments and frustrations. But it is this focus on a life of excellence, which has provided me the ability to overcome those challenges. The pages ahead hold a promise to get you to the same life of excellence with simple elegance.

My desire is to share a simple plan that can be followed by any woman of faith who wants to experience contentment and fulfillment in her home, career and community. By keeping things simple, you *can* achieve excellence and elegance. Life is not easy, but if you can simplify the basic chores of life, you can free up time to go after the dreams and desires God has placed in your heart. And once you begin to see those dreams and desires being fulfilled, you will find purpose and contentment. Many things are not easy, there are few things in life you really enjoy doing that don't require practice to be proficient!

The details outlined in each chapter are personal and often simple, yet when applied, can have a profound impact. By spending your life seeking God's best and aiming to be the best version of yourself, I promise you will find purpose and focus. You will find that, with each season God brings you through, I believe you can "do it *all*," and in that you will find contentment. Striving to aspire to these simple principles of excellence with elegance will bring fulfillment to your life.

In the upcoming pages, I hope you will gain a perspective on your path in life based on my interpretation and understanding of our faith, the Bible and its many lessons and messages. I've interpreted the stories that spoke to me into meaningful messages so that you may apply them to your life. So these words may guide you as they guide me.

For what profit is it to a man
if he gains the whole world,
and loses his own soul?
—Matthew 16:26, NKJV

When the Pursuit of Excellence
is Merely a Pursuit

We live in an imperfect world. Imperfect people. Imperfect careers. Imperfect communities. It is unrealistic to think that our lives will ever be perfect. We make mistakes and, if we aren't careful, our mistakes can result in a life of disappointment.

A Reference in Life

It was the day before Holly was to marry her high school sweetheart. With tears rolling down her face, she frantically called her maid of honor. "I can't marry him. He doesn't love me." The maid of honor, trying to make sense of the disturbing phone call, drove to the bride's home. She found Holly in her bedroom weeping. Holly explained that she felt neglected. "He never pays attention to me. I don't feel loved."

Confused by Holly's claim, the maid of honor assured her that her fiancé did love her. She knew Holly felt he was a little dull, but she reminded Holly that he was kind, considerate, honest, and hardworking. The maid of honor soon realized that this was more than just last minute nerves, so she advised Holly not to go through with the wedding. If he didn't meet all of her expectations, then maybe she shouldn't marry him. However, Holly regained her composure and reassured her maid of honor that it would be fine. She was married the next day.

Life appeared to be good for Holly. She seemed to embrace the life she had chosen. She was generous and enjoyed entertaining friends in her newly built home. She took pride in her job and worked hard to please her employer. Her friends believed that Holly and her husband were in love. Later, when they became the first couple to give birth to a child among their circle of friends, Holly was willing to share the joy. Being a wife and mother was her heart's desire. To everyone who knew her, she seemed to be doing well in her life.

So when Holly asked her husband for a divorce, he was sideswiped. Holly had never communicated her discontentment to him all those years. She wanted more out of life: more money, more excitement and more attention. She assumed she should be at the center of his life without having to request it. She chose to have an affair with an older man of wealth, her boss. He gave her his undivided attention and the security she lacked in her marriage. The whole turn of events came as a surprise to her husband and everyone watching.

But not to me, her maid of honor.

It was clear to me that her needs were unfulfilled. She felt she was meeting everyone else's needs while hers were being neglected. She put the responsibility on her husband first to meet these expectations. But really, she was looking to the wrong person to meet her needs.

Our unfulfilled expectations and unrealistic dreams can overwhelm us with grief and sadness. When we have inflated expectations and dreams, we make meager attempts to fulfill our obligations (in Holly's case, marriage), but typically without passion or zeal. Like Holly, we soon give up because of failed attempts to satisfy the dreams we so desire to live out. It is good to have high expectations for our lives, but if they are misguided goals and we fail to meet them, we are left with no sense of direction or accomplishment. For some, this is heartache too big to bear.

What we have to understand is that situations and people bring disappointment. These shortcomings bring insecurity. As a result, we fail ourselves and others. We can't forgive ourselves, let alone others who have hurt us. In Holly's case, Holly needed to forgive the father who had abandoned her years before, resolve her feelings, and move on with the life she had committed to, all with the help of God. But she didn't.

There will be *seasons of difficulty* for everyone. There are seasons—or stages—of our lives in which we've experienced great challenges and others in which we've enjoyed happiness, blessing, and success. Life's journey is not flawless.

Many times we even look longingly at others' lives and see what appears to be a perfectly wonderful situation, but in reality it is not always what it seems.

A man at our church said to my husband, "Your life is so good. Man, you have a great job, great family, successful business. You've got it made." My husband responded, "If you only knew. God truly has blessed us but we have experienced some things over the last twenty-five years that have nearly torn our family apart. Every day brings a new challenge."

The important truth we need to understand in order to understand the need for God in our life is the following: We are in a world of constant change. *Life is unpredictable*. Like one big rollercoaster ride, careers end, family structures shift and people change. Adjusting our lives to these changes is no easy task. We have to learn to adapt. If we rely on our feelings to dictate our responses to change, we will find that we can't depend on anything or anyone. Even those closest to us will disappoint and let us down. It doesn't take long to realize our greatest need is to have something that is constant and consistent. The conclusion? Hint: The world can't provide it.

Many of us rely on emotions, philosophies, religions, and fads to provide fulfillment in our lives. With fad diets, you lose weight quickly and then gain it back faster. Similarly, we realize very quickly that everything in this world is temporary with no promise of hope. However there was a time when God said it was good and it was perfect.

A Reference in Faith

The first book of the Bible, Genesis, contains the story of creation. Scripture says that God created everything and saw that it was good. The Garden of Eden was the home for the first man and woman. God provided for all their needs and gave them dominion over all living creatures. They had but one rule to obey: God asked that Adam and Eve not eat from the Tree of the Knowledge of Good and Evil. It was a beautiful and enticing tree. Imperfection entered our world when Eve took fruit from the tree. Believing that she would gain wisdom by eating the fruit, she shared it with Adam. Their act of disobedience brought sin into the world.

Eve gained nothing. She allowed jealousy and arrogance to overwhelm good, thinking God was keeping from her that which she thought she desired and was entitled to. Disobedience and selfish desire changed her perfect world into imperfection. As a result she felt shame and insecurity. And as a result of sin, the story continues on in our lives today. We are the same. Our selfish wants and greed destroy all that is good. And it is possible that Eve felt like we often do, that the consequences of our actions are too harsh or unfair.

It is sin and the imperfection it brings into our lives that cause us to feel that *life is not fair*. That life is unfulfilling. For Holly, life was unfair and unfulfilling. Having a father abandon her wasn't fair. But there are many things we experience in life that truly are not fair.

Many of us live life on the premise *that we are victims* having no control of our destiny. Certainly Eve must have felt that she didn't have any control of her destiny moments after the act of disobedience. She could not change the inevitable. We have had moments of helplessness, and have become restless and discontented. We walk day to day just going through the motions, stuck in a routine we don't enjoy. Having reached for a goal and missed it, we sit unfulfilled. We believe the circumstances are too great for us to recover from and we can't return to the happiness we once had. It is in these moments we lose focus and purpose.

What Holly failed to realize was that her expectations and dreams for the marriage were unrealistic. Her young groom could not fill the void her father had created years ago. The rejection she felt as a little girl from his abandonment was still painfully there. Holly longed for the love, security and attention that every daughter desires and should receive from her father. What could have changed this situation? Holly certainly couldn't go back and change the events of her life, but she could have changed her response to them.

Just like the rest of us, Holly had a hole inside. Where hers was the lost love of a father, ours may be the betrayal of a friend, an abusive parent, or feelings of failure. We need to acknowledge that pain and address the wrong behavior that we have used to compensate for it. We need to acknowledge our need for the repair that only God can do. If we begin to seek Him, allow Him to work, and make some conscious changes ourselves, we will begin to see those holes filled.

We don't need to say goodbye to that happy life. The plan for *Excellence with Simple Elegance* is the answer to finding and regaining fulfillment in your life. Simplifying your day-to-day life and having a workable routine will help you accomplish the basic chores of life, which will lead to more time to tackle the big things that really matter. Achieving personal elegance will allow you to possess the tender, gentle confidence that only a woman can bring to this world. This plan will give you clear direction and focus so your life can have purpose.

It is important that you first have clear understanding of what it means to be *excellent*, to live *simply*, and to possess *elegance*. So let's begin by exploring the definitions of these words.

Ex-cel-lence [ek-suh-luh ns] noun

The fact or state of excelling.
A valuable quality.
State of possessing good qualities in an eminent degree.

Excellence is not perfection. Excellence is not the journey to perfection. Excellence is a commitment to improving oneself with the goal to be the best version of oneself. It is an active commitment to excelling in all aspects of life including physically, mentally, emotionally, and spiritually. Excellence is a standard that is above average. It is a commitment to always moving forward. A woman who possesses excellence is fully aware that her value comes from God.

Sim-ple [sim-puhl] adjective

Free from vanity of humble origin and modest position.
Not complex, sincere, unconditional

Simple is uncomplicated. A simple plan is clear and causes no confusion. To live simply is to be real, honest and to have integrity. To live simply is to have a routine that brings excellence to the surface. To live simply is to have a humble and quiet spirit.

El-e-gance [el-i-guh ns] noun

Refined grace, tasteful richness of design, gracefulness, restrained beauty of style, neatness and simplicity. Highly attractive. Beauty in movement, appearance or manner.

Elegance reflects excellence. Elegance is simple, neat, and appealing to the eye. Elegance shows the true beauty of a woman. Elegance celebrates the femininity of a woman.

For the woman of faith, excellence is a result of establishing core values and knowing what you believe. It is the foundation that you will draw guidance, strength, and protection from in an *imperfect and ever-changing* world. A strong foundation for your life is the beginning to operating in spiritual excellence.

Having a servant's heart is a key to a life of excellence. Life is not about you but the people you serve. When *life becomes unfair* you will draw from the elements of the heart. A heart that will draw its strength from prayer, a heart that pumps from grace, and a heart that flows with forgiveness will be the heart that receives emotional excellence.

We'll discuss how creating a simple, uncomplicated routine makes for smooth transitions from one season to the next. *Difficult seasons* can create complexity in one's life. But these seasons of difficulty don't have to last forever. *We choose to be victims.* We can choose otherwise, but it will require us to possess specific ingredients. These attributes will lead us to mental excellence.

Creating a detailed plan and committing to that plan is goal setting, another important element of excellence. Obtaining the skill of goal setting, exploring your talents and gifts, writing them down and staying the course is crucial in turning around unfulfilled expectations and unrealistic dreams.

Additionally, physical excellence for a woman is obtained through simple elegance. When you grab onto the concept of how precious you are to God, you will find value and fulfillment. You won't desire to seek temporary solutions in *fads, religion, or philosophies*. While your emotions change rapidly and are unreliable for what is good and true, your *faith* will soon become what is constant, reliable and good.

Excellence with simple elegance is attainable. I promise.

I will go where you go, I will live where you live,
your people will be my people, your God
will be my God, I will die where you die.

—Ruth 1:16–17, CEV

The Foundation of Excellence
Faith, Family, Community

As any good builder knows, you have to build a foundation before you can construct a building. The foundation I'm referring to now pertains to matters of the heart.

The first step to attaining a life of excellence is establishing a foundation for the life you desire to live. This is a must! It is the very beginning of a life of excellence with simple elegance. A solid foundation keeps you focused and outlines your priorities. The foundation of living a life centered in biblical principals is constructed in this order: faith, family, and community. Here is where you will develop the spiritual aspect of your life.

A Reference of Faith

Ruth lived in Moab around 1100 B.C. She was a true and loyal friend. She lived her life with tenacity and purpose. This Moabite woman of the Bible is a great example of a woman who had her priorities in order. In her book's four short chapters, we see very quickly how our priorities of faith, family, and community are intended to function together.

As the story opens, an Israelite family, Naomi, her husband, and two sons, had moved from their home in Bethlehem to a neighboring country called Moab. In Ruth 1:4 we learn that the two sons took Moabite wives, Orpah and Ruth, even though they knew, according to their law, Moabites were not allowed to become Israelites. They had lived there around ten years, when we learn that Naomi's husband and both sons died, leaving the women alone.

With the men in her life gone, Naomi decided to return to her homeland, Bethlehem, in Israel. Her daughter-in-law, Orpah, did not follow Naomi, but Ruth did. She made an intentional decision to stay loyal to her mother-in-law, **committing to establish a new foundation for her own life**. Ruth made a heartfelt statement, one of faith and commitment. It was a foundational statement that would set her on a course toward fulfillment and into God's purpose for her life.

> "Naomi then said to Ruth, 'Look, your sister-in-law is going back to her people and to her gods! Why don't

you go with her?' and Ruth answered, 'Please don't tell me to leave you and return home! *I will go where you go, I will live where you live; your people will be my people, your God will be my God. I will die where you die and be buried beside you.* May the Lord punish me if we are ever separated even by death!'" (Ruth 1:15–16, CEV, italics mine).

Ruth is passionate about her intentions and that passion is reflected in her words to Naomi; she even acknowledges her intention to suffer any harsh consequences that would result from her going back on her word.

There is an important connection here that can be made to our own lives. When you have a strong and meaningful foundation and you've made a commitment to stick to that foundation, you will find stability even in the face of whatever turmoil or change may come into your life. Ruth's new life began as she arrived in Bethlehem at the time of the barley harvest. Because Ruth took her responsibilities with deepest sincerity, she made a decision to glean fields. It was customary in those days for landowners to leave the corner of their fields for the poor to pick up or glean the extra grain. She chose to diligently work in the fields of Boaz, a relative of Naomi's late husband and a man of wealth and position.

Most importantly, Ruth was being sensitive to follow where God was leading her. Her commitment was so significant that the story follows her loyalty and faithfulness to the Lord as it opened doors that allowed her to join the people of Israel. Ruth's labor of love and humble living gained her goodwill, not only with her community, but also with Boaz. He knew of the sacrifice she made to leave her own country and care for Naomi in an unfamiliar place. That was how Ruth won the heart and love of Boaz, who later made her his wife.

From this, we take a life lesson: It is our actions and how we live out our life that impacts others. Actions do speak louder than words.

It is amazing how God blessed this common woman, not only into marriage with a man of wealth and position, but also with the birth of a son, whom she named Obed. The birth of Ruth's child brought much joy and honor to Naomi, but the full purpose of Ruth's life was still to be revealed.

> "When Obed grew up he had a son named Jesse who later became the father of King David" (Ruth 4:17, CEV).

In following the path of simple obedience and faithfulness, Ruth became the great grandmother of King David, and out of this family line the Messiah was born. What a heritage! With God, all things are possible and all things truly are orchestrated for His purpose.

As illustrated so beautifully by the life of Ruth, a strong foundation leads to the blessing of the Lord. Building from the ground, up, is as simple as making a conscious decision to live by biblical principles (putting God first), then faithfully committing to the ideals of family and community. You will experience this kind of fulfillment and purpose when you choose a life of excellence.

There are three foundations for excellence: faith, family, and community. Let's talk about each one.

✳ Faith ✳

"I will go where you go, I will live where you live; your people will be my people, *your God will be my God,* I will die where you die" (Ruth 1:16, CEV, italics mine).

A simple, foundational statement leads Ruth to a life of purpose and fulfillment. Note the three points of sacrifice Ruth gave to this commitment: *she left what was comfortable, took on great responsibility, and maintained a willingness to be obedient.* This sacrifice demonstrates her true dedication and love to her number one priority, God.

It is human nature to desire comfort. It's easiest to walk through life never facing challenges or difficulty, but it is not best for us. God appreciates the efforts we make to step outside of what is comfortable in order to be obedient toward Him.

A Reference in Life

I remember one such time in my life. I was ten years old and sitting comfortably with my family in the church pew on a warm summer evening. At the close of the service, our pastor invited anyone who wanted to make a commitment to put God first in his or her life to come forward. He mentioned that everyone was welcome but only those who were really choosing to live for God should respond. My heart pounded loudly and tears filled my eyes. My whole body felt restless. In that moment, I clearly saw that I had a heartfelt need only God could fill. The Holy Spirit was urging me to leave my seat, walk forward, and make a commitment to Him. I did. I left what was comfortable to acknowledge my love of Jesus, taking a public stand to show my commitment.

The first-time commitment to God is always significant and memorable. However, it is our constant demonstration of this commitment consciously and on a daily basis that shows our obedience. We must commit and recommit to our foundation, despite our natural inclination to default to what is familiar and comfortable; only then do we become true creatures of God.

In 2 Corinthians 5:17, it says that if anyone is in Christ, he becomes a new creature. All of the old nature is gone, and all things become new. For the believer, the tricky part is walking out that "newness" each day. Every day, we must wake up and say 'Yes' to putting God first.

"In everything you do, ***put God first***, and He will *direct you* and crown your efforts with success" (Proverbs 3:6, TLB, italics mine).

Three Questions

At this time, I asked myself three questions, and I encourage you to do the same:

1. Am I willing to *move out of my comfort zone* to accomplish God's best will for my life?
2. Am I willing to *take on the responsibilities* that come with a life that is passionate for God?
3. Am I willing to *be obedient* to His call and His plan for my life?

If you can honestly say 'Yes' to all three questions, you have just laid the foundation for a life of excellence. You have facilitated the development and evolution of the elements, the building blocks of your foundation. Now the provision of God's *guidance, strength, and protection* is available to you.

Hang on to this promise: God's constant presence is available to you when you put Him first. Wherever you go and whatever you do, listen for His voice. When you are willing to step out in faith into *unfamiliar circumstances,* God's presence in your life will give you *guidance.*

Living Outside Your Comfort Zone: What to Expect

There likely have been times in your life (and there likely will be many more) when you have been faced with an opportunity that takes you out of your comfort zone. You feel that you're being called to something, or an opportunity or need is unattended to and weighs on your mind heavily. This could manifest in a number of ways: A relationship that needs your attention or a challenging opportunity at work. When you feel God is calling you to do something, follow Him outside of your protective world and hear His message to you. As if He's saying, "I have something bigger for you"; He knows you have a desire for something in your heart. This is an important opportunity for many reasons.

While it's no secret that living outside of your comfort zone can put you on edge, there is a reason you have been presented with this opportunity. Don't be surprised if you feel some apprehension or insecurity. Everything is new, so you might find that you are not quite as confident as you usually are, but this is exactly where you can learn to lean on God's guidance and counsel. He is the strength that guides you when you are weak. You will see God work mightily in your life, because you have become reliant on Him. And don't ever forget that you have immediate access to God through His Word, prayer and worship.

WHEN OUTSIDE OF YOUR COMFORT ZONE, FOLLOW YOUR GUIDE

The Bible will be your daily guide that will navigate you to a life of excellence. Sometimes making the commitment to have God first in your life is not easy, while *keeping* Him first is even more difficult. Having a daily routine of reading His Word and praying keeps your mind renewed with what is good and holy, even if it's just 20 to 30 minutes a day! Every bit of time we set aside to meditate on Him will help to shape us into His image.

> "This also comes from the Lord of Hosts, Who is wonderful in counsel and excellent in guidance" (Isaiah 28:29, NKJV).

It is your choice to walk in His guidance and counsel. We will talk more about prayer later on, but know that you have a continual, direct connection to God through your prayer life. The need for prayer is important to understand first, because the guidance and counsel you receive from it will follow you throughout your entire journey.

A Reference in Life

I used to think that I would have to be on my knees or in church to pray and worship God. But as life got more complicated I realized that I needed Him more often. I like to grab quality time with God when I am by myself driving, working on the farm, doing housework, or riding my bicycle. I have even been known to read or pray while waiting in line for my favorite morning coffee drink. I talk to God as though He were sitting right next to me, because He is. God will give counsel when you are willing to give Him your time and attention to listen.

HE WILL LEAD YOU

Every time you make any decision, big or small, seek His will. But be prepared that the right choice for your life may not be the easiest choice to make, but the right path will always be in line with His word. You might not always be able to see the full scope of God's plan, which can be scary at times. Sacrifice and extending yourself beyond your comfort zone is all part of the experience that comes along with your newly established foundation and your commitment to follow His path. The act of obedience may be as simple as rearranging your schedule for the day or putting your desires aside and others' first. It is with these acts of obedience, you will find such freedom, joy and tremendous peace of mind to your soul and spirit just knowing that you are in God's will. You do have the choice to make your life one that has *purpose. His* purpose.

A Reference in Life

My husband and I had just graduated from college and were both searching for jobs. It was my desire to stay in the big city where the university was, but Paul really wanted to move back to our hometown. We sought God's will for our life. It was a big decision. Circumstances seemed to be pointing us homeward, but everything inside of me wanted to stay in the city. It became very clear that God truly was leading when both of us acquired jobs back home that were suitable to our field of study. My husband was delighted, but it took me a while to digest our new direction.

I made the initial choice to follow His guidance (my first commitment). It was the right choice, but not easy for me to accept. Since then, God has blessed and given us great purpose and contentment here. However, complete fulfillment did not come until I was willing to reissue my trust in God consistently, and believe that He knew where I would be my best self. Trust in Him that He knows what is best for us. Until we operate in His will for our life, we cannot be in tune to our gifting—our talents, our anointed spiritual gifting.

A Reference Rooted in Faith

Ruth, like many of us, probably had a dream and a life all planned out in her mind in her home country of Moab. It is possible her first husband was the perfect man to make her life wonderful and fulfill all of her dreams. But when her circumstances changed with the death of her husband, she made the decision to walk in faith and showed her willingness to follow the guidance of God's will. This decision gave God an opportunity to work in her life.

. . . .

God offers the same to you and me, but only with our obedience. His Word will give clear direction needed for a life of excellence. Know that God has a wonderful plan for your life. Making the right choices will launch you into God's will, and into a life of excellence.

WHEN MET WITH A CHALLENGE: A PARALLEL IN FAITH AND IN LIFE OF RESPONSIBILITY AND STRENGTH

"God is all *strength* for his people" (Psalm 28:8, MSG, italics mine).

With commitment comes great responsibility. In those *responsibilities,* God provides *strength.* Spending all day in the fields and being mindful each evening of a distressed mother-in-law's needs had to have brought exhaustion and weariness to Ruth. As women we, too, have a broad range of daily responsibilities: career, community obligations, household chores, children to love, and a husband to adore. It's difficult to imagine how to accomplish these responsibilities on our own, let alone perform them with excellence.

I believe that one of the greatest opportunities for God to demonstrate His manifested strength in someone's life is in the period following the loss of a child.

A Reference in Life

A friend of mine, Janice, shared with me the deep, overwhelming sadness that had entered her heart just hours after her nineteen-year-old son was killed in a motorcycle accident. During the week of the memorial and funeral for this great university athlete, Janice was kind, consoling, comforting, concerned, caring, loving and unselfish. *She is handling all of this with such grace, I thought.* She was a tower of strength for all who came to mourn his death.

I knew of her strong faith in God, but I was not the only one. She was aware of her faith in God and relied on it during this time. Others asked about her demonstration of strength, and she openly shared that God was her provider. Tears ran freely that week, but through them there was confidence and strength that God was in control. Janice could take the responsibility of providing comfort to others because she had a God who stepped in to become the provider of her strength.

When responsibilities and circumstances cause weariness, hold on to the promise of Psalm 29:11: "The LORD will give *strength* to His people; the LORD will bless His people with peace" (NKJV, italics mine).

Where we are weak, He is strong. God's presence in our lives gives the strength and confidence to handle all of life's responsibilities.

"And this is love: that we walk in obedience to his commands" (2 John 1:6, NIV).

WHEN OBEDIENCE BECOMES
A PART OF YOUR TOTAL COMMITMENT,
YOU WILL HAVE ACCESS TO GOD'S LOVING
PROTECTION IN ALL YOUR PURSUITS.

We see it in the second chapter of Ruth. In verses 11 and 12 we read the conversation that Boaz had with Ruth. "I've heard how you've helped your mother-in-law ever since your husband died. You even left your own father and mother to come and live in a foreign land among people you don't know. I pray that the LORD God of Israel will reward you for what you have done. And now that you have come to him for protection, I pray that He will bless you"(CEV).

Ruth needed it desperately, and so do we.

God's provision of support and protection is revealed in verses 15 and 16:

"When Ruth gets up to start picking up grain, Boaz says to his men, 'Don't stop her, even if she picks up grain from where it is stacked. Be sure to pull out some stalks of grain from the bundles and leave them on the ground for her. And don't speak harshly to her'"(CEV).

"Know this: *Your God-honored life is tightly bound in the bundle of God-protected life*" (1 Samuel 25:29, MSG, italics mine).

Ruth's physical needs were met in abundance. Her emotional needs were met with the provision of companionship from other women. God's protective canopy is for those who remain obedient and faithful to Him, and He will apply that protection to every area of your life.

"God's your Guardian, right at your side to *protect* you" (Psalm 121:5, MSG, italics mine).

A Reference in Life

Being a parent of children serving in the military, I hold to this promise tightly. Acquaintances are always curious about how we feel as parents of a fighter pilot. "Are you not frightened for his life?" they ask. While we are very much aware of the danger, our commitment to step outside of what is comfortable and follow in His path puts me at peace. It is important to remind yourself that God has called each of our children into their careers, with varying levels of danger and intensity, and because they've been faithful to that call, our children are in the center of His will for their life under His divine protection.

His protection is not just for the physical needs of our family members, but extends to their emotional, mental, and spiritual protection.

Physical protection. God's canopy of protection will keep you from physical harm and illness so you are healthy to complete His purpose and His will in your life. Proverbs 29:25 says, "But whoever trusts in the Lord shall be safe" (NKJV).

Emotional protection. God's canopy of protection will keep evil far from you, and also keep you from bringing hurt and trauma to those around you. John 10:28–29 says, "And I give them eternal life, and they shall never perish; neither shall anyone snatch them out of My hand. My Father, who has given them to Me, is greater than all; and no one is able to snatch them out of my Father's hand" (NKJV).

Mental protection. God's canopy of protection will keep you in wisdom and bring clarity in decision making. Scripture also says that when we keep our minds on Him, He keeps us in perfect peace. He has not given us a spirit of fear, but of power, of love and of a sound mind (Isaiah 26:3 and 2 Timothy 1:7, respectively).

Spiritual protection. God's canopy of protection will keep you sensitive and on the path to living according to His Word and truth. Knowing what is good and right leads to a life of holiness. Psalms 91:12 says, "He ordered his angels to guard you wherever you go. If you stumble, they'll catch you; their job is to keep you from falling" (MSG).

SHARING THE FAITH

God is faithful about meeting your needs. He has given you these promises so that you may live life boldly. The commitment to a godly life will be a daily decision that will give you direction and focus. Chase after God's will for your life daily. Step out of your comfort zone, handle the responsibilities with confidence, and be completely obedient laying aside your agenda to seek God's.

Your act of faith and being in His Word daily leads to understanding His will for your life. Understanding His will gives purpose for this earthly life. This established foundation delivers the guidance, strength, and protection needed for a life of excellence. Your life is no longer about your needs and you; it's about sharing God's love.

A Reference in Life

Little more than a year ago, God brought a new friend into my life. I know when this happens, He has a special purpose. Donna, a professional, 30-something woman in our community appeared to be living the ideal life of excellence. She was highly visible in community events, in her line of business, and socially. She was always dressed to the hilt and beautifully put together. Petite, cute, sweet and adorable. Her words were always kind and encouraging, smart and well spoken. She was also a good communicator who was much respected in the business world—where she worked nearly 55 hours a week. And, her house was immaculate.

As an acquaintance, I was drawn to her. I remember thinking, "God, what could I possibly bring to Donna's life?" It was a mistake in my thinking. As it turned out, it wasn't me that would add to her life, but what God wanted to do through me. He knew she needed an older friend like me. He also knew Donna's future held some major physical struggles. She attended our church several times and, as our friendship developed, God made me aware that, spiritually, she was seeking. I invited her to a women's event at our church. That night, Donna made a commitment of faith. The world around her would attest that she appears to have it all together but she will tell you that, without God being first in her life, there had been no clear direction or purpose. But with her acceptance of Him, and her building of this new foundation for her life, God has made her life complete. God showed her that He is bigger than this physical struggle she was experiencing and He has become the guide for her life.

You don't have to know all of the answers; you just have to know the One who does.

❊ Family ❊

"I will go where you go, I will live where you live, ***your people will be my people***, your God will be my God, I will die where you die."

From Scripture we know that God considers family of utmost importance. To further support it, He refers to Himself as Father and to us as His children. It's a simple and beautiful way to underscore the value He places on familial relationship. Our heart should beat with the desire to sacrifice self in deference to service to our family.

A sincere commitment to make *your family the first priority above all human relationships is the second step in building the foundation that leads to a life of excellence with simple elegance.*

Let's reflect again on the story of Ruth.

A Reference in Faith

"All that you say to me I will do" (Ruth 3:5, NKJV).

Ruth's daughter/servant role to Naomi, her mother-in-law, shows the beauty of family commitment. It's not hard to see from her actions that Ruth placed a high priority on personal relationships.

The sacrifice of hard work gleaning fields, and her humble, obedient spirit brought her into position for bigger things—God's purpose for her life. Like in Ruth's case, we, too, can find great blessings from learning to relate to others as Ruth did, especially in her commitment to Naomi.

As women, we need to desperately pray that our desires lend to this kind of loyal, servant heart. Women, we need to put our family and their needs before all other human relationships, and sometimes even our own. Unfortunately society (even the church) has not considered the necessity of nurturing intimacy, communication and commitment within the family. With the high demands the earthly world has put on women, we have stripped away the gentleness of who we are. We are pushed by outside influences that are very much of this world to be so independent that we become hard, cold and resist our gentler instincts.

A Reference in Society

According to recent studies by the Barna Research Group:

- 11% of the adult population is currently divorced.
- 25% of adults have had at least one divorce during their lifetime.
- Divorce rates among conservative Christians were significantly higher than for other faith groups, and much higher than atheists or agnostics.

According to organization president George Barna:

While it may be alarming to discover that born-again Christians are more likely than others to experience a divorce, that pattern has been in place for quite some time. Even more disturbing, perhaps, is that when those individuals experience a divorce, many of them feel their community of faith provides rejection rather than support

and healing. (Dec 1, 1999, www.religioustolerance.org
Ontario Consultants on Religious Tolerance.)

By glancing through the numbers, we can quickly ascertain that
something different needs to be done. There needs to be a fresh
approach to marriage and family. That change can start with us. Let's
first address the attention we give to our children and our husbands.

Among the greatest human needs is one of genuine acceptance. No matter what our age, we long for the approval of our
parents. This acceptance, or the lack thereof, often determines
how we view ourselves and affects our ability to love our children, our spouses and our friends.

A Reference in Life

My boys and husband have always been the center of my world.
I've always loved them deeply, and I believe I've always had a servant heart when it came to family. Each member of my family
had huge dreams and aspirations—from fighter pilot and sec-
retary of defense to financial officer, stock broker and owner of
a private jet service. While I wanted to encourage all of them, I
didn't know exactly how to go about it. From my perspective,
they were all so out of reach. Because of this, I made a concerted
effort over the years to seek any source that could give insight
into raising them. I tried to get my hands on any tool that would
help me to express my love and admiration, while not squelching
the dreams God had given them.

The Blessing

In the late 80s, I came across a book by Gary Smalley and John Trent called *The Blessing*. The authors believe that many people spend a lifetime looking for the acceptance that the Bible calls "the blessing." In this book they capture the ideals of parental acceptance.

Smalley and Trent explain the concept of 'the blessing' by going deep into the traditions of the orthodox Jewish home and observing their pattern of being passed from generation to generation. In the Old Testament, the focus of the blessing was on the unique spiritual and prophetic aspects, including the material inheritance. Today the Jewish home has adopted the basic relationship elements of "the blessing" to communicate acceptance and affirmation to their children.

The authors identify five keys to passing on the blessing in our families:

- *Meaningful Touch*: Hugs, kisses, physical, intentional, sincere love expressed through touch.
- *The Spoken Word*: Words of kindness, acceptance, and admiration.
- *The Expression of High Value*: Words and actions that show honor and value.
- *The Description of a Special Future*: Using words that give pictures of a special future for the one being blessed.

- *The Application of Genuine Commitment*: Understand that you as a parent have a responsibility and an active role in making their special future come to pass. "Words alone cannot communicate the Blessing. They need to be backed with a commitment to do everything possible to help the one blessed be successful." (Taken from *The Blessing*, 29.)

These five elements became the tool that I used to enhance the way I communicated love and acceptance to my boys. Bestowing the blessing was a model of behavior I wanted to exhibit. So I made a conscious decision to make a daily practice of blessing my children.

I began with a daily routine of giving hugs and kisses to the boys. (This was never a struggle for me because I came from a family that freely gave hugs. So, meaningful touch was already incorporated into our life with morning, greeting and 'good night' hugs.)

I then consciously added random out-of-the-blue kisses and hugs, or 'just because' embraces. It was in those moments that I also included a kind word, keeping in mind that it was for the boys' benefit and not mine. Sometimes, because of our own insecurities, we express love with a touch or kind word in hopes of getting something in return. We have to be on guard about this, otherwise we are aiming to meet our own needs instead of giving the blessing to someone else.

The elements of meaningful touch and kind words are expressed to fully meet the need of the one to which you are bestowing the blessing. They are acts of selflessness. We already know the Golden Rule that comes from Luke 6:31: We should treat others the way we would like to be treated. So many times we get caught being selfish. We say unkind words. We hold back on a meaningful touch because we feel victimized by our own children, spouse and friends.

I have been guilty of this very thing. I have spoken harshly in an unjust situation. The disappointment of the person's actions, I thought, justified my actions and unkind manner (certainly not what you would label Christ-like). And to this day I regret those moments. I thought I *needed* to be right. But you see, it is better to be righteous than right.

We need to step back before we attack. We need to listen and wait for His direction. God will give you the strength to be righteous instead of humanly right. The best thing you can do is keep the big picture in mind. Don't get caught up in those small, ugly moments. Don't let circumstances and actions of others dictate your response. Those are the moments you want to tap into the strength that only God can give.

The next part of the blessing is the expression of high value. This one takes a particular amount of work and creativity from the giver. It is so true that to receive respect you must show it. Especially with children, we must be mindful that they have value and need to know that you honor them. You want to recognize each accomplishment. Be truly engaged in endeavors. Don't miss important events in their lives. The need remains even as the child becomes an adult. Their self-esteem is built partly on how you value and respect them. They need to know that you are proud of them.

Next, communicating the elements of genuine commitment and a special future are shown through your time and financial commitment. I believe these two walk hand in hand. The authors gave an excellent example of this in their book. To speak into a child's life that he would be an incredible pianist (special future) but then not buy him a piano (no commitment) makes no sense.

Your children do have a special future. God has a wonderful plan for them. Jeremiah 29:11 in The Living Bible says that the Lord "knows the plans He has for you. For good and not for evil, to give you a future and a hope." We all have wonderful dreams for ourselves. God is the one who places those dreams in us.

It is no different for your family. They have dreams and need you to be a helpful visionary with genuine commitment to see them become a reality. This means *acting* upon all that you have *spoken* to them. It is a physical/financial commitment *and* an emotional commitment. They need to know that they have your support and blessing in their endeavors of life. Every parent falls short of this sometimes. Did I? Absolutely. And so will you, but each morning renew your mind to intentionally serve your family in this manner.

Exercising the elements of the blessing can be the source of communicating approval—not just to your children, but to your spouse and others as well. The authors even encourage adults to extend the blessing to their parents. (The life of Ruth is an excellent example of an adult child extending the blessing to a parent.)

If you are constantly striving to release the blessing into the lives of those around you, you will be operating with loyalty and commitment to your family. It is this servant heart that will lead to the excellence God has for you.

Marriage

I cannot have a section on family without addressing the marriage relationship since the marriage is the center focus of family. A husband and wife who walk in unity and mutual respect for each other is God's intentional design for marriage.

> "Wives, submit to your own husbands as to the Lord" (Ephesians 5:22, NIV).

> "Husbands, go all out in your love for your wives, exactly as Christ did for the church—a love marked by giving, not getting" (Ephesians 5:25, MSG).

Really, my husband has the hardest job here: Loving me as Christ loved the church. And what did Christ do? He gave his life for the church. Men are to lay their life down for their wives, loving them all out, and women need to simply walk beside them in quiet confidence, respect, love and honor.

Many women cringe when they hear the word *submission*. I'll elaborate on my thoughts on the topic. I think of myself as a strong woman—not helpless by any means. When I think of submission to my husband, I view it as this: I made a really good choice in the man I married. This walk with him has been wonderful. I am so thankful for the man I chose to walk beside.

In our church, the bookstore always features a book of the month. One particular month the featured book was *The Shack* by. William P. Young. I rarely read fiction, but when my friend and the director of our women's ministry, Lesa, strongly recommended it, I thought I should read it.

What I found fascinating was the author's perspective on relationships, primarily the relationship between God the Father, Jesus, and the Holy Spirit. The protagonist, Mac, could not grasp how submission operated within the unique relationship of the Trinity. And from conversation about this topic in the book came this quote, "Submission is not about authority and it is not obedience; it is all about relationships of love and respect" (*The Shack*, 145).

That is it. The heart of submission is filled with love and respect. Look at Ephesians 5:21 from *The Message*, "Out of respect for Christ, be courteously reverent to one another." And even more specific, the NIV says it this way, "Submit to one another out of reverence for Christ." God is asking us to be submissive—courteously reverent—to one another out of our extreme love of Him.

In view of that perspective, let's look at submission under these three points, which I call "the three points of submission in a marriage":

1. Quiet Confidence
2. Mutual Respect
3. Love and Honor

The first point is having a quiet confidence in your husband's leadership. How do you build this confidence? How does this confidence occur? Confidence is developed when success has been experienced. Ideally, confidence is built into the relationship during the courtship. If you are reading this book and you are single, please hear me when I say, "It's in the courtship." If he hasn't won your confidence while you're dating, having confidence in his leadership in your marriage can be a constant struggle. Life is easier when you make good choices for yourself. And it is certainly true when it comes to choosing your life partner.

A Reference in Life

My husband and I were high school sweethearts. I loved being with him. He made me laugh, took me on fun dates and always respected me. I quickly gained confidence in him. He worked hard and was very industrious. I was fully confident that he truly loved me and would always care for us in the future. He made good decisions concerning his life and I knew he would do the same in our life together.

Married life is a workout. I will admit this wonderful walk between my husband and I was built with, as they say, blood, sweat, and tears. It is two different people trying to function as one. It is a daily chore for any couple to keep trust in their relationship. Acquiring trust and confidence takes patience and time. The courtship is an ideal time to begin developing that quiet confidence and trust, but it's the marriage where these are nurtured. Putting the effort forward early builds a strong foundation for the marriage. It makes for a loving and lasting friendship.

When we marry, we have to keep mindful that we didn't marry a perfect person. And neither did your husband. As a wife, you need to take on the biblical responsibility to encourage your husband. Cheer him on! And don't beat him up when he makes a mistake. Being a good leader takes time to develop. We all make mistakes and the words of "I told you so" just don't belong in our vocabulary. God asks us to love our husbands unconditionally, which will bring unity and tenderness in your marriage.

Secondly, submission comes when you experience respect in a relationship. Respect the position that God has placed your husband in. He is to give leadership in the marriage. Work on having mutual respect for each other. Don't try to control. Submission is not dominance, but partnership. My advice is to walk beside your husband and be a loving support for him, allowing him to lead. The best thing you can do for your husband, whether he is walking in his place of leadership yet or not, is this: Be proud of his accomplishments, and always speak well of him. You have a lot of power with your words to encourage him and build him up to be the man God intends him to be.

A Reference in Faith

First Peter 3:1 reminds us, "Wives, likewise, *be* submissive to your own husbands, that even if some do not obey the word, they, without a word, may be won by the conduct of their wives" (NKJV, italics mine). Find contentment in his leadership and do everything you can to support his continued growth.

A Reference in Life

In our courtship, mutual respect began to develop when we took the time to become best friends. Time was the best advocate for developing the respect needed for a loving, lasting relationship. We took the time and energy to know each other's hopes, dreams and desires. Time allowed me to learn to respect the things he had a heartbeat for. Time gave me the opportunity to understand the values and the passions that motivated this man. During this time, I truly fell in love with my best friend. To this day, I still feel the same; I would rather be with my husband than anyone else. Submission is made easier with the atmosphere of respect.

We have now arrived at the third point: love and honor. You can honor your husband by loving him until it hurts. The scripture says to never let the sun go down on your anger. My husband says in our relationship, we don't let the sun go down on our anger; we just stay up until dawn. Frankly, I hate disharmony. After more than 30 years of marriage, we have had our moments of intense disagreement. But I have made a commitment to listen to my heart during those moments; I never stay angry more than a couple of minutes. My heart always reminds me how much I truly love and adore this man. Mentally, the disagreement is then put into perspective so that my love and honor wins out. Women, do this. Your reward will be great in heaven, even if your earthly reward isn't.

A woman of excellence has quiet confidence in her husband's leadership, respects him, and loves and honors him until death. Even when it isn't easy, never give up. Stay the course of excellence in your marriage relationship. It is never too late to develop these attributes in your marriage.

✳ Community ✳

"I will go where you go, *I will live where you live,* your people will be my people, your God will be my God, I will die where you die."

A Reference in Faith

"Love your neighbor" (Mark 12:33, NIV).

A Reference in Life

Aubrey was an eighth grader when we met. She had made some bad choices that caused her temporary expulsion from school. The superintendent of the school district, my husband, provided a tutor for the completion of her academics at home and also asked me to be her mentor. Aubrey had it rough at home. Her parents were divorced, her father struggled with alcoholism and her mother was a victim of a circumstance, which pushed her to a personal struggle. Her siblings had fallen into that same downhill spiral of dysfunction.

I remember the first thing my husband said to me concerning Aubrey. "She is a sweet, good kid. She is a good student who has potential. I believe Aubrey could turn her life around if you would be her life coach." I never said 'no' to any of his referrals.

This tall, slender girl was always wearing a smile and she won my heart. She possessed the same love for ice cream as I do, so the local Dairy Queen was always our first stop before we began our extensive talks about what her life could look like in ten years. As a mentor/life coach it was my responsibility to assist her in a routine that would help her become healthy, feel valuable and be successful.

Because I am a firm believer that you must meet the physical needs of a person before you can even begin to address any emotional need, a shop-til-you-drop adventure was at the top of the agenda. New attractive/appropriate clothing and fun girly stuff would help give her a feeling of confidence. And, it was a legitimate need. Most of the clothing that lay on the floor in her tiny bedroom at home was too small. After working to meet some of her physical needs, the only thing left that she needed was God in her life.

A window of opportunity to share the love of God came within the first month of our get-togethers. She had a warm response to God's Word. When I told Aubrey that God loved her and had a wonderful plan for her life, she was encouraged. She expressed the desire to have God's best for her life.

Aubrey soon embraced the Christian faith. It became the foundation for her life. She loved attending church and reading the Bible. Each time we met, we would pray that God would grant guidance, strength, and protection. At church she felt love and acceptance she had never experienced. She felt safe there. The friendships made at church were valuable. She made sure that I took her to every service or event that our church offered. Her routine was simple: outings with me, church, and eventually she was back in school.

Within our third year together, Aubrey made a decision to move from our community. Life at home with her mother had further deteriorated, and she knew she needed to leave, even though leaving her friends, teachers, and church family would not be easy. She decided to move two hours south to her grandfather's home. Immediately she embraced a new church, new friends, new school and a new outlook on life. Her goals were in place. Her dreams of college and a career kept her focused. She allowed no distractions to get in her way.

Aubrey's faith in herself and her God kept her on a path of success. She went from familiarity to the unfamiliar with confidence that God would provide her guidance to a fulfilled life. Aubrey just finished her first year of college and is well on her way to fulfilling her dreams while living out her faith. She is confident that her future is bright.

Being Aubrey's mentor has totally convinced me that we can positively affect our community one person at a time. Matthew 5:14 tells us that we are to be a light, bringing hope where there is no hope. There is a lifestyle that shines for God. We need to have a lifestyle that makes time for others, adding value to others, and loving them.

Community should matter to you. *The commitment to community is the third step in building the foundation that leads to a life of excellence.* Utilizing your career and community service can be your outreach or mission field that will give you a platform to put your foundation and faith into action. Having a job also affords you room to challenge yourself, to exercise your God-given talents and to share God's love.

Our lives are so full of opportunities and demands that striving to maintain proper priorities is essential. There is a place for God, a place for family and a place for the host of other things that take us out of the home. Having a career, serving in your church, and being active in your community can bring so much more fulfillment to your life when you are first mindful of your priority to God and family.

Living these parts of your life outside of the home can serve to remind you of a grand scheme. You really do matter in the sum of life, and are part of something bigger. Find value in it, and remember that each job or act of service is God's way of preparing you for bigger and greater responsibilities. Purpose will be everlasting if all pursuits are done with God First—a legacy that has lead others to God's guidance, strength, support, protection, and love and will continue to do so. Your commitment will also allow others to experience God's love and touch when you allow God to use you. Again, your life will no longer be about your needs, but about sharing the precious love of Jesus.

Raising children, marriage, career, church, charity work, community... Every aspect of our lives can be changed for the better with a pure motive of unselfishness. When you commit to furthering His Kingdom in your local community, in turn you will receive fulfillment and purpose—a demonstration of God delivering favor and blessing to you.

In the book *Beyond Jabez*, Bruce Wilkinson speaks about actions to be aware of while performing service to your community. He says, "Watch the way you treat people, listen to your tone of voice, pay attention to whether you become pushy, be sensitive to how well you listen to others' opinions and stories, go practice mentorship." It may be difficult, but it is crucial to continually ask yourself these types of questions:

- Is this community better because of my presence?
- Are people blessed because they know me?
- Have I touched others and my community positively?
- Am I the light in the dark moments for others?
- What has God called me to do?
- I don't only represent my family and myself; am I acting as a direct conduit of God's love?
- What characteristics of mine draw others to God?
- What if my life is the only Bible some people ever read?
- Am I actively exhibiting the fruits of the Spirit? Love, joy, peace, patience, kindness, goodness, faithfulness, gentleness and self-control?

In your serving of others, remember the words of Dr. Bill Anderson, "God did not call us to have lots of friends, but to be a friend."

A sound heart is life to the body.

—PROVERBS 14:30, NKJV

The Heart of Excellence
Woman of Prayer,
Simple Grace, Simply Forgive

God created each of us uniquely and loves us just as we are. He is, however, most concerned with what 1 Peter refers to as the 'hidden person of the heart'. Because He understands that out of our hearts flow the issues of life, He has a way of equipping our *hearts* for each season of our lives. There are three specific **God-given elements to the heart of a woman of excellence: prayer, grace, and forgiveness.**

Having a servant's heart is a key to a life of excellence. When *life becomes unfair,* you must draw from the elements of the heart. A heart that draws its strength from prayer, a heart that pumps from grace and a heart that flows with forgiveness will be the heart that receives emotional excellence.

A Reference in Life

Most of the seasons in my life before the age of 35 had been fueled and energized by people. I saw no purpose for quiet solitary moments, eating alone or doing anything completely by myself. My energy came from people. I was an extrovert! Then, God called me to a season where I was to find value in quiet times. This meant that my physical-emotional-mental-spiritual being was going to be fed in silence, grounded in quiet moments of prayer and worship. God used these times to impress upon me the elements that help us to prepare for each season of life: Prayer, Grace and Forgiveness.

✳ Becoming a Woman of Prayer ✳

Adjusting my prayer time to quiet moments alone was *so* out of my comfort zone. Looking back, I see how my life was similar to the struggle of Martha from Luke 10:38–42.

A Reference in Faith

"Jesus entered a village. A woman by the name of Martha welcomed him and made him feel quite at home. She had a sister, Mary, who sat before the Master, hanging on every word he said. But Martha was pulled away by all she had to do in the kitchen. Later, she stepped in, interrupting them. 'Master, don't you care that my sister has abandoned the kitchen to me? Tell her to lend me a hand.' The Master said, 'Martha, dear Martha, you're fussing far too much and getting yourself worked up over nothing. One thing only is essential, and Mary has chosen it—it's the main course, and won't be taken from her'" (MSG).

Just like Martha, I had found more value in the *service* of God and others than in the intimate moments of simply loving the Lord. What He really desired of me was the heart of Mary; intimacy with me, but also to prepare me for tough times ahead. God wanted me to become a woman of prayer. I was introduced to this simple format of A.C.T.S. for prayer, and it revolutionized my prayer life:

Begin prayer with *adoration*, a time of praising God for who He is, His attributes, His name, and His character. I had no idea how to begin, but He led me to use the Psalms, read them to God; praise Him through the words of David. So simple!

Move on to *confession*. Confess your sins and ask for His forgiveness. According to 1 John 1:9, "If we confess our sins, He is faithful and just to forgive us our sins and to cleanse us from all unrighteousness" (NKJV).

Next spend time in *thanksgiving*—blessing the Lord. Psalm 61:8 says, "So I will sing praise to your name forever, that I may daily perform my vows" (NKJV).

And finally, *supplication*—your prayer list.

A Reference in Life

The voice of prayer that was modeled to me as I was growing up was always formal and in King James Version. Some of the prayers were remote and memorized. It was hard for me. I was embarrassed to pray out loud because I knew in my heart that my prayers were not eloquent. I viewed my prayers as common talk and assumed they were not honorable to such an awesome God. I also seemed to get caught up in giving God my want list. "God please do this, help me with this, get me this…" On and on it went. As I matured, I realized this certainly could not be pleasing to my God.

The A.C.T.S. truly enriched my quiet time, worship, devotional and prayer life. In these seasons of solitude with God, He was preparing and equipping me to be able to handle anything, while showing me how I should seek Him. I urge you to use this prayer format to enrich your own prayer life.

A.C.T.S. gave me freedom to have a common everyday conversation with God. In scripture we are reminded that He refers to us as His children, so then, of course we can talk to Him as a father. It only makes sense that we approach Him lovingly and honestly like He does with us. When we take time to know and hear His voice, we find out that His words to us are spoken in everyday language we understand. It doesn't matter if you are praying out loud in a group or in private, make your conversations intimate, loving and honest.

A.C.T.S. also gave my personal quiet time prayer more depth and meaning. It helped me to become more focused on being thankful instead of needy. When we take time to honor God for whom He is and to praise Him for all He has done, our adoration of Him will grow even more. A prayerful heart is a thankful heart.

I have found a prayer journal to be a great help. This does not have to be a long and tedious process. Pick out a small notebook. Write down your supplications/make a prayer list. Don't be afraid to petition the small things along with the big requests. Watch how God works and answers. Then weekly go to your journal and write the answers to prayer requests down. Being able to see exactly how God has worked in your life will not only develop in you a thankful heart, but also help you to thank Him for meeting all your needs.

Routine and habit is the key to excellence in prayer. Make it a habit to take God with you everywhere you go; don't leave Him out of anything. Prayer is not dictated by place and time. Its place is everywhere; its time is any time. Make this your mantra. In the last chapter I discussed the need to have conversations with God more often—not just during my quiet times. I began optimizing my time and talking to him more frequently I realized I needed His presence desperately when I was alone, so I decided to listen to worship and praise constantly. Music helped me with this process, having a way of ushering me into worship and prayer. In order to understand the importance of prayer in your life, it's necessary to realize that prayer is powerful. I've experienced God's ability to move on my behalf through prayer numerous times. It is not difficult to find spiritual truth and direction for life's challenges. All we need to do is ask God for direction, look for it, and trust His promise to provide it. Yes, it can be difficult to have the patience to be at the mercy of His timing, but remember that His timing isn't ours.

A Reference in Life

As a business owner, I've had many opportunities to learn this hard lesson. With our business of farming Christmas trees, our income happens just one time a year. It can be especially challenging to budget revenue to meet the needs of the growing season and to make it last throughout the season. Timing is everything. This is where I have learned to pray with a different request.

Being completely aware each year what my income would be, what I had to sell from the fields and the market price each year, my prayer would have a twist to it. I would ask that my expenses would be less instead of asking God for more.

At the end of the growing season one particular year, money got really tight. Even though my first inclination was to panic, I trusted that God knew of my need; I was confident He would provide because I had used wise judgment with spending. I knew we would be cutting it close in the following month, and it would be a challenge to meet the financial demands of the farm. Within days of this notable concern, I received a substantial refund check in the mail from our insurance company that had been delayed (in other years we had received it in the spring, but this year we didn't receive it until late summer). I had otherwise forgotten about it. God's timing was perfect. The amount met my need for the month. It certainly wasn't coincidence; it was the provision of God and His answer to my prayer.

God is a faithful provider to those who are obedient to His will. Matthew 6:8 tells us that God knows our needs and our desires even before we ask, and in the very next chapter (7:7) he tells us that all we have to do is ask and it will be given. Never underestimate the power of prayer.

⚹ Simple Grace ⚹

"For by grace you have been saved through faith and not of yourselves; it is the gift of God" (Ephesians 2:8, NKJV).

Grace is a showing of kindness, favor and blessing motivated by love in a situation where it is undeserved. God's grace has been extended to us. Our salvation is by His grace alone. Through His grace He meets us where we are, giving us liberation *from* law and *to* become who we are supposed to be in Him. Living in God's grace gives us the ability to live the abundant life He so desires for us. It is here we experience His unconditional love and freedom to live. Grace makes "holy living" possible during times of our life in which circumstances and character are so attacked by the world and sin.

According to the *New Spirit-Filled Life Bible* (Kingdom Dynamics, 1556), there are four main roles of the grace of God.

First, God's grace restores us to wholeness. It repairs and perfects. Next, it establishes a solid foundation and grounds us securely in the truths of His unconditional love. Thirdly, it provides the ability to stand firm, causing His strength in our inner man to live triumphantly. And lastly, it brings the blessedness of His "rest" and the fullness of His promises. Our salvation is a free gift; it's God's goodness even though we don't deserve it. All we have left to do is receive. Grace and the power of God in your life are what move you to excellence.

In Charles Swindoll's book *The Grace Awakening*, he tells us to watch out for the grace killers that might cross our path. Religion and legalism put the "dos and don'ts" into play; they are the enemy of a living and active faith. Legalism puts unrealistic expectations and works into our faith. We must embrace the idea that we are choosing to live in holiness because of the awesome respect that we have for our God. Grace came to us through the Cross. It is through Christ's death and resurrection that we have salvation. This forgiveness is from Him alone, not by us trying to do something to earn it. And what liberty comes from extending this same grace to others!

In our maturity, we learn to be less critical and more tolerant of others. According to James 4:12, we are not qualified to judge anyway: "There is one Lawgiver, who is able to save and to destroy. Who are you to judge another?" (NKJV). Ultimately we should be spending our time loving others and showing tremendous kindness. Grace should be our pursuit and our passion.

A Reference in Life

My husband has what I like to call a "yes face." When we were raising our boys, he said "yes" to their requests as much as possible, and for that, he always seemed so approachable and positive to our sons. If the boys asked to play outside when we had other commitments, he would say "Yes. We just have to finish up our other commitments (whatever they were) and then we can play outside." He'd use this answer instead of "No, not right now," because he wanted the boys to feel confident and hopeful when approaching him. In turn, when we did say, "no," the boys knew we truly meant it. Of course he would encourage me to do the same, always reminding me to say "yes" as much as possible to our boys' requests. Many times it took me a little creativity to have a "yes" answer, but even if I could not grant the request right at the moment, I would try to think of an opportunity sometime in the future that I could. Because of this, they never hesitated to bring their petitions to their dad. He was approachable.

Similarly, this is true for our heavenly Father. With the outpouring of God's grace even when we are undeserving, I believe that God also shows us He has a "Yes face." With His constant grace and forgiveness, He has shown us that He is approachable,

He invites a relationship with us, He wants for us to come to Him with our deepest concerns and requests and He says "yes" whenever He can—if not right now, then maybe in the next season. He says simply, "Ask and you shall receive."

Romans 5:1–2 says, "We have peace with God through our Lord Jesus Christ, through whom also we have access by faith into this grace in which we stand, and rejoice" (NKJV). We should mimic our Father, who conquers by lavishing His love upon us with a "Yes face." His grace is (more than) sufficient.

First John 5:3 in *The Message* says it this way:

> "The reality test on whether or not we love God's children is this: Do we love God? Do we keep his commands? The proof that we love God comes when we keep his commandments and they are not at all troublesome."

This scripture tells us that the proof of loving God is keeping his commandments. I can think of several tasks that are made easier because we do them for people we love: cleaning toilets, running kids to soccer practice, laundry. This is the same with keeping God's commands. No matter what He asks of us, no matter how uncomfortable we may feel when He calls us out of our comfort zone (or how unsavory the people are that He asks us to love!), if we truly love Him, we will obey.

The beauty of obedience is that experiencing His grace and His love in return makes whatever sacrifice we made appear small in comparison. His grace and the power of God in your life are the vehicles that drive you to the place of excellence.

✳ Simply Forgive ✳

Forgiveness is not a feeling, but a decision. A life of excellence comes with a forgiving heart.

In Mark 11:25, Jesus gives us clear instructions: Whenever we pray, we are to forgive, "But when you are praying, *first forgive* anyone you are holding a grudge against, so that your Father in heaven will *forgive* your sins, too" (NLT, italics mine).

Everyone makes mistakes; because of our human nature, they are inevitable. It's the way we deal with them that makes the difference.

So many people make mistakes that they regret for the rest of their lives. Without a doubt, that's why God created forgiveness. He made a way for us to start anew—a way called Restoration. Job 33:26 says, "For He restores to man His righteousness" (NKJV). It is never too late to set your path straight. Begin resetting your foundation on biblical principles today. There's no better time to get your heart and house in order. That place is where freedom lives.

But remember, choosing a life of faith and living it in excellence always comes with sacrifice. You may even have to sacrifice things like position, prestige, or relationship. Living a life of purity and integrity means you will not be loved by all.

In his book *Get the Junk Out of Your Trunk* Pastor Duane VanderKlok stresses the importance of forgiveness and daily prayer, as taught by Jesus to His disciples. Let's look at this model prayer found in Matthew 6.

Beginning with, "Give us this day our *daily* bread," Jesus leaves no question of how often we should pray. This means we daily come to Him in prayer to first *forgive* those that have hurt us. Then in verse 12 He continues: "Forgive us our sins just as we have forgiven those who have sinned against us." Refusing to forgive others is too high a price to pay. The act of forgiveness grants us the privilege of being forgiven by our heavenly Father.

How often should we forgive that person who did us wrong? Scripture spells it out in simple math. Matthew 18:22 says we are to forgive someone, seventy times seven times, which equals 490 times. The message here isn't to literally forgive someone 490 times, but the spirit of this instruction suggests that no matter how many times someone wrongs you, you keep on forgiving.

Just as forgiveness sets you free, a lack of forgiveness creates resentment that will eat away at your life. We cannot allow the feelings of resentment and bitterness to grow or, before we know it, these feelings will occupy our minds and interfere with our ability to build our foundation and reestablish our commitment to God daily.

In VanderKlok's book, he warns us that bitterness will rob you of the joy that would normally be experienced with your

family, friends, careers or blessings that God has for you. But forgiveness allows you to let go of the hurtful events of the past and
gives way to freedom so you may take hold of the bright future
that God intended for you to have. God did not give us life to
just endure, but to enjoy abundantly. In John 10:10 Jesus said,
"I have come that they may have life, and that they may have it
more abundantly" (NKJV).

A Reference in Life

I had really messed up. I was bent on being "right" and had spoken some harsh words. I came to a point in my life in which I
had to ask for forgiveness. It wasn't easy because I hadn't forgiven
myself. I had carried this burden for too many years. I asked the
person whom my words fell upon to forgive me, and reluctantly
she did. Immediately I felt freedom from a heavy burden. Even
so, my heart told me that with prayer, she would truly forgive
me, and our relationship and bond would be healed.

There have been times when I have suggested to others that
they just needed to forgive the person who had wronged them.
Their immediate response was, "I don't think I can." Remember,
forgiveness is a choice. You *can* make a conscious choice to forgive. Trusting that person again may take time, but forgiveness
only takes a moment.

Somehow we have the idea that when we forgive, we are
doing something wonderful for the person we are forgiving. In
reality, forgiveness for others is what's best for ourselves.

A Reference in Faith

I encourage you to follow Apostle Paul's advice in Philippians 3:13: "I am focusing all my energies on this one thing: *Forgetting* the past and looking forward to what lies ahead" (TLB, italics mine).

And finally, Ephesians 4:32 says: "Be kind to each other, tenderhearted, *forgiving* one another, just as God through Christ has *forgiven* you" (NLT, italics mine).

Be a woman of excellence with the foundation of God's incredible *grace, prayer, tender heart, and forgiving spirit.* When we live out these attributes and trust Him to come into our lives, those around us will begin to see less of us and more of Him.

Whatever you do, do it heartily,
as to the Lord and not to men.
—COLOSSIANS 3:23, NKJV

The Ingredients of Excellence
Courage, Passion, Discipline

ecoming a woman of excellence is like following a recipe. There are specific ingredients that we must possess if we want to be the best version of ourselves. These ingredients cause us to make good choices and will lead us to mental excellence.

A WOMAN OF EXCELLENCE

God has called us to excellence. One might find the task of creating and maintaining a life of excellence to be a daunting one, and it *can* be if we do not understand most importantly that excellence is a journey. It is not, however, a journey *to perfection*.

Perfection will never be obtained here, only strived for. Excellence is a level of existence above average and a standard we can aim for and obtain.

A Reference in Life

I'd always found a challenge in serving family meals. I have never claimed to be a gourmet chef—just a mom cooking the family's favorite recipes. When my kids were growing up, I never really made anything all that fancy, just regular dishes that were often repeated. The truth is that I just didn't want to put the extra time in to be creative or excellent. Some women choose to hire a housekeeper at some point in their lives; I, however, wanted a chef! It takes time, energy and willingness in this journey to achieve excellence and to acquire the ingredients that comprise it.

Once you've established that you are on a journey, it's important to realize what it will take to get there. In this journey you will need **these three primary ingredients: courage, passion, and discipline.**

✳ Courage ✳

When considering the topic of courage, I stumbled upon this quote in the *New Spirit Filled Life Bible* that sums up the direction we should go. "Know that God grants seasons of favor for His people in order to extend His kingdom. Press in to God for all that He has for you in these seasons, and give Him all the glory" (Truth-in-Action, 643).

A Reference in Faith

Much could be learned about a person in biblical times just by hearing their name. I would like to share the story of Queen Esther. Her name means "star," and her life did nothing less than shine light on the beauty of recognizing a season of favor and God's sovereignty in one's life. Just like He did with Ruth, you will see how God uses a common woman to fulfill a significant purpose of great importance. In Esther 4:14 scripture says she was ordained to fulfill God's purpose "For such a time as this." God works today in our lives the same as He did for Esther, and He's given us stories like her life because He loves us so very much. We can learn from her story because we also have a specific purpose—a plan that is just right for each of us. Let the riveting story of God's shining "star" inspire you to live out your passion and mission.

I have to believe it would have been truly fascinating to live in the same village as Esther, watching her story unfold. She was an orphaned Jewess, adopted and raised by her cousin Mordecai, a leader of the Jews in the Persian Empire which stretched from India to Ethiopia about 5th century B.C. As the story goes, the queen at that time had disgraced the king, so he determined to replace her with a virgin from his kingdom. He sent appointed officers to the provinces to gather all the beautiful young virgins. Esther possessed great beauty and loveliness, and was one of the young ladies taken to the king's palace.

According to custom, all of the chosen ladies were to go through a series of beauty regimen in preparation for their time before the king. Once the beautification was complete, the day came for each one to see him. Each lady was allowed to take whatever item she desired along with her from the women's quarters to the king's palace. But the King's eunuch, the custodian of the women, advised Esther to do something a little different: take nothing along when she went except what he suggested.

What did Esther have over all of the others? I mean, wasn't she just one in a sea of beautiful faces? The answer was her courage, her character, God's sovereignty, and being in the center of His will. You must believe that God has a wonderful purpose for your life, one that is significant and important. Any one of these young ladies could have been a beautiful queen, but Esther possessed all the right ingredients to fulfill God's purpose *for such a time as this.* Found in Esther 2:9, "Now the young woman (Esther) pleased him (the king), and she obtained his favor" (NKJV).

By God's sovereignty and Esther's courage, the door was opened. Verse 15 says that Esther "obtained favor in the sight of all who saw her." She could have taken whatever she desired with her as she presented herself to the king, but she heeded wisdom. She thought for herself, showed great strength and courage—characteristics that came directly from her commitment to God. As a result, "The king loved Esther more than the other women, and she obtained 'grace and favor' in his sight more than all the virgins; so he set the royal crown upon her head and made her queen" (Esther 2:17, NKJV).

If the Cinderella story had ended there, it would still be a remarkable example of God's ability to elevate us when we make a decision to honor Him. But she took a step beyond the fairy tale and into an even greater real life story when she shined brightest as darkness entered her life as Queen.

The lives of her people, the Jews, became threatened. Up until that point she had kept her Jewish heritage a secret in obedience to Mordecai's request. But now, Mordecai gave her something new to think about. He told her that without intervention, she and her family would perish, and posed the question, "Who can say but that God has brought you into this palace for just such a time is this?" (Esther 4:14, TLB). Mordecai was actually calling Esther to her mission. Realizing that she may be the only hope of saving her people, she and Mordecai decided that she would have to make a request of the king.

Do you have someone in your life that challenges you to seek out your destiny? Do you have someone who is motivating you to discover your significant life-mission? If not, let this book be the beginning of that inspiration.

In Esther 4:16 she prepared by telling Mordecai to "Go, gather all the Jews who are present in Shushan, and fast for me; neither eat nor drink for three days, night or day. My maids and I will fast likewise. And so I will go to the king, which is *against the law, and if I perish, I perish!*" (NKJV, italics mine).

This woman was not only incredibly courageous, but smart and obedient. It is remarkable that she was willing to risk her own life for the Jewish people. She definitely believed that God—not her beauty—had given her the position as Queen.

It took great courage to act as Esther did. Sure she had prayed and asked others to as well, but to actually go through with the plea was another feat. (So many times we are willing to pray and to seek His counsel, but not to actually take action.)

In those days, it was improper to approach the king unless he had summoned you. To violate that protocol put you at risk for death. In chapter 4:10 and 11 Esther told Mordecai, "All of the king's servants and the people of the king's provinces know that any man or woman who goes into the inner court to the king, who has not been called, he has on law put all to death, except the one to whom the king holds out the golden scepter, that one lives. Yet I myself have not been called to go in to the king these thirty days" (NKJV).

What Esther did next reveals that she was not only beautiful, she was also very bright. She didn't share her requests with the king in the courtyard; instead she planned a party—something she knew he loved. She actually made the king wait. This was an ingenious plan. Esther knew this would pique the king's interest, putting him completely at ease and in a perfect place to hear her petition. This plan worked to her favor. Look at Esther 5:1–2, "…Esther put on her royal robes and stood in the inner court of the king's palace, across from the king's house, while the king sat on his royal throne in the royal house, facing the entrance of the house. So it was, when the king saw Queen Esther standing in the court, that she found favor in his sight, and the king held out to Esther the golden scepter that was in his hand." (NKJV) What Esther didn't understand at the time was the measure of God's incredible favor on her life. Sometimes we doubt that God could possibly give us that much favor here on this earth.

I am sure at that moment she breathed a huge sigh of relief and said in her heart "Thank you God!!" At the well-orchestrated dinner party, she courageously reveals her heritage to the king and pleads for protection on behalf of her people. Because the king loved Queen Esther and saw her courage and honesty, he honored her petition.

Courage was the motivation deep in the heart of Esther. She displayed it in various ways. We first see her courage in the form of strength. She left a safe, comfortable place and moved herself to an unknown environment. Just like Esther, God can truly move in our lives when we are willing to get out of our comfort zone and become completely dependent on Him for all we need. Have the courage to place your future in God's hands. I believe each one of us has that strength, if we are willing, to risk big things for God.

The second form of courage demonstrated in Esther's life was a willingness to live in submission and obedience to authority. For Esther, it was the king's eunuch and Mordecai, her cousin who had raised and loved her like his own daughter. If you look back into the story you will remember she took the advice and counsel from these two authority figures. We must have a willing and submissive heart to those in authority in our lives. Be open to wise counsel, and obedient to God's call on your life.

The third form of Esther's courage was sacrifice. She beautifully demonstrated a willingness to give up her personal agenda for God's agenda, despite any discomfort or danger that her obedience may have cost her. By trusting God's sovereignty in our lives, we may also experience discomfort, criticism, and ridicule. Following His plan for our lives may never put our lives in danger, like it did for Esther, but it definitely will not come without sacrifice.

Just like He did for her, God will reward you with His favor. Esther's courage resulted in the deliverance of God's people. Your courage will make the difference in your world. The pursuit of excellence isn't easy. You have to be willing to stand alone if necessary. Be the unpopular vote. Do what is right! Be a woman of integrity, someone that everyone can count on, even if it costs you something. Be a woman of action, not just talk. Whether you are on a college campus, at home, or in the work force, stand up for what you believe is true and good. Walk with a purpose and go the extra mile.

✳ Passion ✳

Webster's New Collegiate Dictionary says that *passion* is a strong liking for or devotion to some activity, object, or concept. That means it's an object of desire or deep interest. It is often that our deep interest might change with different seasons of our life. Learn to be flexible and explore new passions.

Love what you do and do what you love.

A friend once told me to find what I had a heartbeat for, and serve there. When you find that place, you will find that it's also where your passion lies. God has called all believers to serve others. It is imperative to develop a "servant heart." When you realize that life is not about you but others, life begins to simplify.

Esther realized just that. God had positioned her as queen so she could have influence that would ultimately result in the deliverance of the Jews. She had a heart that sought God's purpose in lieu of her own self-interest. Passion was displayed to the max with her willingness to lay down her life for her people.

For Esther there were definitely times of anxiety and uncertainty, as is the nature of leaving one's comfort zone. Her life and the lives of the Jewish people were at risk of being annihilated by their enemies, even by order of the king. Even though her situation seemed hopeless, Esther's passion for her *people* and for her *purpose* kept her faithful. Like Esther, passion can give you that drive to continue when it appears all hope is gone. God will not forget your acts of service. He will bless you, and His plans and purposes will continue to go forth. Like a domino effect, passion and service can lead to contentment.

A Reference in Life

My husband and I share the same passion. Our passion for family, church, community, and school (and making them all work together) is exciting. This passion even led us to choose careers that incorporate all four. Where we serve tends to always be at the center of our passion in some capacity. A simple rule of thumb is to serve where it makes sense and at the capacity for the season you are living in. For example, when I was raising my children, I was heavily committed to ministries for children and young moms at church. Being committed to serve there met my emotional, physical, spiritual, and mental needs, thus leading to contentment in that specific season. As director of several children's ministries, instructor of a women's aerobic class and leader of a women's prayer group, these opportunities fit with the priorities that I had established in that season for life: Faith—Family—Career. And it made great sense to serve God in a place where I could bring my children with me.

Choosing what is best for your family, not just your career advancement, is a huge sacrifice that can be very difficult. I was fortunate enough to be able to apply this principle to my professional life as well. It was a luxury that I will be forever grateful for. When you seek to fulfill His will for you in that way, God can enable you to live out your passion in a fashion that you would never have imagined.

A Reference in Life

While growing up, I never really had an interest in reading. Because I was a relatively slower reader, I easily became distracted and disinterested. But as you know, reading is a required activity for academic learning, especially in college. In my desire to develop my personal quiet time with God, a passion for reading finally developed. I found a passion for books, and a love and appreciation for excellent writing.

When an opportunity arose to work in our student media center, I took it. I had so much fun learning a new skill of librarianship and had another opportunity to be with children in a quiet setting (what person wouldn't jump at a chance for quiet?).

Passion allows endeavors of life to be enjoyable, fun and creative and takes away the mundane repetitive motion of just doing the work. If you can harness that strong feeling toward the endeavors of your life, you will find joy, contentment, and fulfillment while developing commitment. Make sure your passion starts strong and remains strong to ensure you're not only a great "starter" but also a great "finisher" at achieving excellence. Without passion, commitment is weak. But passionate lives are great lives!

Ephesians 6:7 should be the mantra of the Woman of Excellence, "Work with enthusiasm, as though you were working for the Lord rather than for people" (NLT). Because, guess what? You are!

❋ Discipline ❋

According to *Webster's New Collegiate Dictionary* the word *discipline* means "orderly, prescribed conduct or pattern of behavior."

Even after you have set a format for your life that lines up with God's Word and will, it is not always an easy path to stay on. Life provides hundreds of opportunities that challenge us to look at our decisions, to evaluate and adjust. In short, a life of excellence takes discipline.

Having clear dreams and goals within the format of your life can give you great momentum and direction. Choosing to sidestep boundaries by making a wrong choice because it appears easy and gratifying can be short-lived and painful. The decisions we make for ourselves will affect us our entire lives. **If our goal really is excellence, we need to be prepared to stay the course.** In 1 Corinthians 9:24 and 25 we see that the person who wins the race is the one who practices discipline:

> "Do you not know that in a race all the runners run but only one gets the prize? Run in such a way as to get the prize. Everyone who competes in the games goes into strict training. They do it to get a crown that will not last; but we do it to get a crown that will last forever" (NIV).

From the thirty-first chapter of Proverbs we learn what a virtuous and disciplined lifestyle should look like for us as women. This passage says of the virtuous woman:

> "Her worth is far above rubies. She *does good* for her husband and not evil. She willingly *works with her hands* and *provides* food for her household. She *considers* a field and buys it. Then from her profits she *plants* a vineyard.

She *empowers* herself and *strengthens* her arms. Her lamp does not go out by night. She *stretches out her hands* to the spinning wheel and her hand holds the spindle. She *extends her hand* to the poor and *reaches out* her hands to the needy. Her household is clothed with scarlet and she even *makes* tapestry for herself. Her clothing is fine linen and purple. She *makes* linen garments, *sells* them, and *supplies* sashes for the merchants. Strength and honor are her clothing. She *opens her mouth with wisdom*, so her tongue is the law of kindness. She *watches* over the ways of her household, and does not eat the bread of idleness" (italics mine).

I believe we need to make a life-altering decision to be this disciplined. From the virtuous woman we see the necessity of developing a pattern of behavior of discipline that exhibits *hard work*.

The author of Proverbs plainly spells it out: *This* is what a hard worker looks like.

Did you notice the phrase, "Her lamp does not go out by night"? My friend, please hear this—a woman of excellence gets up early and works past dark—with "strength" as her clothing. She is productive and orderly, while exhibiting wisdom and kindness. Idleness simply isn't her style. The excellent woman realizes that her boss is her heavenly Father and she does everything as unto Him. But among her favorite things about hard work is that it leads to success and vacation.

To become a woman of excellence, we must apply discipline to each area of our lives, and be prepared to stick with it, no matter how long it takes. We don't always get the results we want right away, but discipline helps us to be faithful while we wait and change. This is especially true in the area of prayer. Like a farmer who plants his crop and tends to it, sometimes our labor of prayer produces results in another season of our lives. It is also seen clearly in the realm of parenting.

One of the most difficult and beautiful parts of the journey toward excellence is that this ability to be disciplined unfolds over time.

A Reference in Life

There is no doubt that, as a mother of three boys, I consistently needed to be a woman of patience and discipline with prayer and grace. During my teen years, when I would dream and plan out my life, it was always my desire to be a wife and mother. It truly can be a rewarding career in itself. What I didn't realize then, is that you are a mother for life. I thought that when your children turned 18, you were finished.

Was I naïve or what? Sometimes your life's work, your children, take you into worlds that you would have never gone to—some good and some not so good. There are days where I am totally exhausted because of praying for my sons. It feels like I have just run a marathon!

Similar to the discipline and patience parenting requires is in my physical line of work. Our family operates a Christmas tree farm in Northern Michigan.

Farm work is one of the most difficult jobs physically. As if long hours and the operation of equipment that is both physically draining and emotionally taxing weren't enough, we are also very vulnerable and dependent upon weather that we can't control. As a Christmas tree grower you put a lot of faith in the yearly labor practices and routine maintenance that it will produce an excellent product at harvest. Unlike other types of farming where planting and harvest are the same year, the Christmas tree is planted about 7–15 years before it is ready!

On the farm, we have a piece of farm equipment called the Mankar. It is very important to kill the grass and weeds that grow naturally among the Christmas trees, so we spread herbicide to accomplish that task. The herbicide is applied as a fine mist spread evenly across the field. Continuous application results in good soil with no weeds. This also enables the Christmas tree to gain full benefit of irrigation and rainfall. Like most farm equipment, the use of the Mankar is very labor intensive. As you spread the material, Roundup, you wonder if the labor you are enduring will produce the desired result. The results cannot be seen for up to three weeks.

It's the same with your children. A child that you have consistently and gently poured your life into might not flourish or be established for 30 years. Just like removing the weeds, consistently loving, affirming and disciplining your children will help to remove undesirable behavior. Being disciplined and patient with prayer is an important part of living in excellence here. Regardless of how taxing a particular season of your life is, we must stay disciplined (like in our role as parents) even though the result may not occur until far into the future. But that result is well worth the discipline, patience and hard work. Remember the encouragement from Galatians 6:9, "And let us not be weary in well doing: for in due season we shall reap, if we faint not" (KJV).

A Reference in Life

The tree farm also brought the opportunity to learn what hard work and discipline is to our sons. Before he entered high school, our youngest son (who weighed no more than 90 pounds soaking wet) showed me an important lesson about discipline and perseverance. One Saturday, the dreaded job of basal pruning needed to be done on a particular field of Christmas trees. To get the job done that day, our son invited several of his middle school buddies, mainly football players, over to help.

I thought certainly they would know what hard work was and would be able to accomplish the job in a day. This simply was not the case. Our son out-performed them two to one, proving that it's not what you are made of on the outside that creates discipline and perseverance in a person, but what you are made of on the inside.

So what did our son possess that the others didn't possess? Ownership and passion. Because he was personally invested, he'd cultivated a heart for performing the task with all that he had inside to give. It motivated him to push past the pain and discomfort to accomplish the job well, whether or not an audience was applauding him through it. The same is true for you. Anything you touch or do has your name on it. How you do something reflects on you and who you are. You need to take ownership of your life, be passionate, disciplined and patient and do it well. Take pride in all you do in life. When you invest your heart, you'll be amazed at the results.

Our lives will be enriched when we exercise the qualities of courage, passion, and discipline. Just as a child who lacks discipline is unruly, it is difficult to incorporate discipline in our lives when they aren't anchored in healthy routine and obedience. If we are patient and diligent with what God has entrusted us, nurturing it the best we know how, we will grow into women of excellence. We will become mothers who love their children with their lives, wives who live dedicated to their husbands, and wonderful examples of what God can do with a passionate and courageous life!

There is a time for everything, and a season for every activity under heaven: a time to be born and a time to die, a time to plant and a time to uproot, a time to kill and a time to heal, a time to tear down and a time to build, a time to weep and a time to laugh, a time to mourn and a time to dance, a time to scatter stones and a time to gather them, a time to embrace and a time to refrain, a time to search and a time to give up, a time to keep and a time to throw away, a time to tear and a time to mend, a time to be silent and a time to speak, a time to love and a time to hate, a time for war and a time for peace.

—ECCLESIASTES 3:1–8, NIV

Seasons of Life

Understand the Seasons, Prepare for the Seasons, Purpose for the Seasons

O riginally written by King Solomon and later commemorated in popular music and poetry, this Old Testament scripture reminds us that there's a season for everything, from emotions to activities to work. On one hand, these words are a sobering reminder that nothing lasts forever; while also encouraging us to remember that difficult times will eventually be followed by times of tranquility. They challenge us to look at history and at our own lives from a grander perspective. God is definitely in control of it all, and nothing occurs that He has not already included into His plan.

✳ Understand the Seasons ✳

Like the seasons of nature—winter, spring, summer, and fall—so are the seasons of life. Seasons are specific periods of time, and they vary in length. Some seasons last for a period of years while others can be just a few short months. It's important to note that the opportunities of one season are not always available in another season.

Additionally, each season prepares us for the next. Just like the foundation we've spoken of, every season depends on the one before. If we don't do our job to prepare, whether by lack of obedience or discipline in a particular season, we won't enjoy what God has for us in the next season.

We all have a number of desires that we feel need to be fulfilled. But what is important to remember is that God has an appointed time or season for each desire to be fulfilled. Some desires can be reached all in one season, others cannot. The best way to avoid feeling overwhelmed is to respect that you can't do it all *all of the time*. When we recognize the seasons we are in, and exercise wisdom in them, we can experience all that God desires for us in that season.

Seasons are birthed out of three specific reasons. The first is the natural *sequence or chapters of life*. Our development has a progression made up of increments of time containing specific experiences. For example, the increment of time called childhood is carefree and fun loving for most children, lending to play, creativity, imaginative thinking and dreaming of what will be. We develop our likes, dislikes and most likely our passions during that season. The responsibilities of childhood are considerably less than those of adulthood, but aid in preparing us for the different task of adulthood.

Each chapter—childhood, adolescence, young adulthood, adulthood, and senior years—holds first-time experiences that make these seasons unique. The "sequence of life" seasons are generally the same for each individual, but the experiences within these appointed seasons could be extremely different. This is due largely in part to personal circumstances and the choices one makes.

Parenting is a good example of a time-appointed "sequence of life" season. Giving birth and parenting is physically easier at a certain time of life. It doesn't mean it can't happen past the comfortable time, but it makes the most sense to have children when you're younger so you can spend more time and energy raising and nurturing them. This means that this particular season is only available to us for a certain period of time. So if we want to experience what God has to offer us within this season, we must enter into that season at the appropriate time.

Secondly, seasons can appear in our lives because of *specific, monumental events*. Some of these events are anticipated and some are not. Examples include graduations, a birth, the death of a loved one, moving to a new address, a new job or career or even a significant birthday. These events can create seasons that bring with them a rush of emotion. Sometimes, even when we know they are coming, they can affect us in ways we wouldn't otherwise expect.

A Reference in Life

The memory of the morning I turned 50 is not a joyful one. It was the first time I woke up with tears in my eyes because I would have to celebrate my birthday. All I could think about was how I was now on the downhill side of my life. I felt old. I had to decide whether I would let my age define me, or if I would adjust to this new stage with grace.

How we decide to live after these monumental events, and how much we let them affect us can have a significant impact on the quality of life we experience after them. They can present monumental change for good, or stunt us.

The last type of season can seem a little more incidental, when in truth, they are not incidental at all. I am referring to the seasons when God is working a *specific purpose* in our lives. Even though He is always speaking and drawing us to Him, there are appointed periods of time that He is aiming to help us grow in a specific area. He is developing our character. It is during these times that He reveals unique truths to us, shaping us more into the image of Christ. He allows them to happen to bring us to a specific purpose.

These seasons are sometimes recognizable when we seem to hear the same Scripture verse every time we turn around, or we keep finding ourselves in situations that reveal a certain character flaw that needs correction. Sometimes they even happen as a result of our prayers for wisdom or patience. He affords us these (sometimes subtle) opportunities to grow. These seasons seem to appear out of the blue and without order, but that is part of learning to trust God and not lean on your own understanding.

❊ Prepare for the Seasons ❊

It is our human nature to hang on to some seasons, even when God is ready to move us to another one. New seasons can bring fear, discomfort and feelings of inadequacy because they typically take us out of our comfort zone. Trust that God has prepared you for the next phase of your life. There will most likely be challenges in the seasons to come, but you know there will also be rewards.

A Reference in Faith

Psalm 37:4 says "Delight yourself also in the Lord, and he shall give you the desires of your heart" (NKJV).

A Reference in Life

The struggle to move into a new season happened to me about 10 years ago. My husband had been a schoolteacher by day, and a Christmas tree farmer in the evening for years. But when he was offered and accepted the role of superintendent in our school district, it left no time for Christmas tree farming, the very practice that was part of his life since childhood. Although he would have no time for the trees, we weren't ready to give up our farm.

The solution was simple: I would become manager and co-owner. Over the years, between raising our sons and pursuing my profession, I had farmed with him on the weekends. Because I adored my husband and loved to be with him every moment, I had acquired a working knowledge of Christmas tree farming. I had also already been handling the paperwork, payroll, and marketing for the business. Now that the boys were older I thought, "I can do this."

Little did I know that my farming career would eventually bring local, state, and national recognition to me as a woman in farming! All from an unexpected season of life! Remember, God knows the desires of your heart. Just be obedient and faithful.

I would like to be able to tell you that life's seasons flow seamlessly from one into the next. In a perfect world you graduate high school, go to college or straight into your career, get married and have children. But seasons don't always happen in that order. Should seasons not flow from one to the next, life may get complicated. An unexpected season (for instance, having a child before you establish your career) does not necessarily come from making poor choices; sometimes seasons shift as a result of good things too. The sequence of life does not always happen in our ideal order—but it can still have a good ending. It is how you respond to that season no matter what it is and how you live within it that can bring great fulfillment.

A Reference in Life

For instance, most of my life's milestones happened at wonderfully inconvenient times. In high school, I was focused primarily on music and academics in preparation for college, when Paul came into my life. Years later, we were thrilled at the birth of our first son, although he was born before Paul had a teaching position and before we had a house.

Life takes unexpected turns, so we need to keep our focus on the Lord, and the goals we know will not change. We need to prepare for the future, but really *live* in the moments we are in. If we will let Him, God can show us how to be our very best self in each of these seasons. If we are, however, unwilling, whether by lack of self-confidence or not trusting that God can make us proficient and adequate for what lies ahead, we can miss great opportunities.

A Reference in Life

I would like to share a little story of a time I failed to have confidence, and almost missed one of the most incredible opportunities of my lifetime. In 2008, *Progressive Farmer Magazine* chose the 10 best counties within the United States to live based on the criterion of clean air, clean water, affordable farmland and general quality of life. Our county was placed sixth on the list.

Subsequently, the local chamber of commerce was to choose one small, successful family farm as a representative of the county to be filmed by The Weather Channel, and we were fortunate enough to be chosen. This meant that we would spend a day with one of the largest film production crews in the country, one that was typically reserved for shooting extreme skiing and snowboarding. (I knew this because our family sport was downhill skiing and our sons were All-State ski-racers, and Jr. Olympians. The production company was huge in my eyes, as I had watched their films as a young child and later bought their DVDs for my sons to watch.)

When the day came to film the segment, my husband announced that he would be unable to spend the day shooting on the farm. It would just be me. And since I was the one running the farm, it made perfect sense to him that *I* should be on camera. One would think I should be thrilled for this great opportunity to show off our farm. But no. I instantly doubted my ability. I felt inadequate. I couldn't help comparing my small self to this company that was accustomed to elaborate shoots of well-known extreme skiers zooming down the great, snowy cliffs of the Rocky Mountains. How could I possibly measure up?

Satan was trying to destroy that moment in time for me. It was to be God's little reward for my hard work and faithfulness, and I was ready to throw it away, forgetting that He had prepared me through previous seasons just for this opportunity. It was in that turmoil that God showed up. On my drive over to meet the production crew God reminded me it was He Who had done a good work in me. He said, "You have worked hard; just enjoy the favor I am showing you today."

It turned out to be a long but glorious day. Bright sunshine reflected off of the snow-covered fields displaying my evergreens perfectly, just as God had planned. Although I was exhausted from the day, I was so grateful to have spent twelve hours with such an incredible, talented group of young adults. They remarked that the shoot was one of the best experiences they'd had and were amazed at the farm production. Several months later, just before the Christmas holiday, my little farm (and my hard work) was displayed on national television. God, You are so good!

Sometimes when we are waiting and anxious to move into a new season of our lives, it's easy to resent the one we're in. This is especially dangerous because we can miss out on the goodness of life or something extremely significant (for instance, if anxious to move out of the season of life in which child rearing takes place, we could neglect to parent the way that our children need us to). It is so important to embrace and value where we are in our lives and appreciate each stage we go through. It is important to learn contentment in each season, and trust that God doesn't forget the desires in our hearts that we have and have still yet to experience.

How long do seasons last? Seasons will vary in length. Some seasons will be so enjoyable that you will want to stay there forever. While other seasons will be so challenging, you will hope to quickly learn the intended lesson, expedite your stay and move on to enjoy the benefits of the lesson learned.

A Reference in Life

Winter stormed in like an uninvited guest. It hung on and hovered over me like a huge dark cloud. The morning did not welcome me kindly, only with tears and exhaustion. I had decided it wasn't going to be a good day. Today I would just exist. All of the life and happiness that I had known appeared to be gone, never to return. Most people would say I was suffering from depression.

Several weeks passed that way and I finally decided I could no longer go on with this unexplained sadness. I would have to be my own best therapist—no one was going to come to my rescue except me. The next morning, I opened my eyes and chose to be happy. I got myself into a routine to move forward and boost my physical, mental, emotional and spiritual health. I made an effort to focus more on the other people in my life as well. Sometimes the darkness of winter forces us into the arms of the ones we love. It was then that a spring season finally came into my life. You have to make the effort to get out of the winter season of life and jump into the spring season where everything again becomes fresh and alive.

A Reference in Faith

In this spring season I was hungry for something new. God's arms embraced me in a unique way, revealing the truth of 1 Chronicles 4:10, the prayer of a man named Jabez became my heart's own petition: "Jabez cried out to the God of Israel, 'Oh, that you would bless me and enlarge my territory! Let your hand be with me, and keep me from harm so that I will be free from pain.' And God granted his request" (NIV).

Have you ever dared to pray the prayer of Jabez? Just like Jabez, I wanted to be more and do more for God. In the midst of this spring season, I decided I wanted to be bigger for God in all aspects of my life: my faith, my family, and my career. So I embraced this challenge and prayed like Jabez. While soaking up rays in Florida's sun, I soaked in the words of Bruce Wilkinson's book *The Prayer of Jabez*. It was everything I desired. I truly ached for more of what God had for me. I was ready for the full life that was promised to me in the scriptures.

Soon after I began to pray like Jabez, an opportunity to take over an established Christmas tree lot in southern Missouri fell into my lap. A wholesale customer of mine had operated it for twenty-five years, but it was now available to me.

Oddly enough, having a lot in the South had always been a dream of mine. The climate at this tree lot was perfect for selling trees in December, not too cold and not too hot. I was thrilled for the opportunity to meet people of the community who had been buying my trees for years. What I didn't know at the time was that God was also giving me an opportunity to boldly share my faith.

During that year, there was a big debate about whether to continue referring to the evergreen as a Christmas tree or to begin calling it a holiday tree. Nationwide chain stores wanted to change the name in hopes of persuading buyers of all religions (or no faith at all) to purchase trees, and embrace the tradition of this evergreen centerpiece.

A gentleman I knew through the business heard that the regional news station wanted someone to speak on this matter from a Christian perspective, and he recommended that I represent the business. Within a few days, a TV crew came out to the lot, shot the interview, and aired the piece during several broadcasts throughout the week.

Who would have thought I would be given a free platform to share about keeping Christ in Christmas *and* that it would happen at the beginning of my first selling season in Missouri? The timing was so unique that I knew it was a direct answer to my request to "be bigger for God and His purpose." God had answered my petition *and* expanded my territory right before my eyes.

❉ Purpose for the Seasons ❉

As women, we often have an innate need to be able to do and be many things. You *can* be a great wife, mother, successful in your professional life, in your service to God at church, and a dependable community volunteer. But recognize that there is an order to maintain, and a specific season in your life to do it.

You have to be ready for each season by being organized and disciplined. Each season gives you great knowledge, wisdom and opportunity to be educated for what lies ahead in your life. Just like building up from a foundation, your experiences prepare you for the coming stages of your life. Don't miss any season in your life, as that will also be an *opportunity* missed. You'll find that these opportunities are God's purpose for these seasons.

Certainly there are many opportunities that come knocking on your life's door, so how do you know if one is right for the season that you're in at the moment? If it is keeping you awake at night and you can't stop thinking about it, go for it.

Ask yourself these three things:

1. Does it line up with God's principles?
2. How will this affect my family?
3. Is this a once-in-a-lifetime opportunity?

If it lines up with the foundation you have set for yourself, go for it.

In some cases, you have been praying and seeking God for an opportunity. Other times it is so far out of your comfort zone, you have to wonder if it is even God who is pushing you to make that positive leap!

Reference in Life

Take this book, for instance. Thoughts kept jumping into my head—a word here, a story there—and I knew I needed to write them down. The feeling was so persistent; I knew God was calling me to this opportunity. Why? I wasn't asking for this opportunity to write a book. I told God, "This is totally outside of my comfort zone." Then my husband mentioned something to me about sharing in some manner either written or spoken (opportunities always seem to arise) some of the same thoughts that had been invading my brain, but I hadn't even spoken to him about them. How did he know what was monopolizing my mind? Soon after that, I heard a sermon that finally drove it home to me. God captured my attention and revealed so plainly that *He* would continue to give me the words and provide me the assistance. So I began to write.

It is so necessary that we stay keen and look for the right opportunities for the season. God brings new experiences in these seasons that enrich your life and add value to it. He also uses seasons to fulfill the secret desires that you have put aside and not yet fulfilled in your lifetime.

A Reference in Life

My secret desire was music.

Music has always been a huge part of my life. Through high school and the first years of college, I pursued performance as a bassoonist. I enjoyed every opportunity to play. But a season came where I had to put it aside, believing and praying that it would be a part of my life again someday. I even turned down an opportunity to play in a professional orchestra. It was a sacrifice, but my decision was simple; it wasn't best for my family at that moment. The commitment was great and would take me away from my first commitment: family.

A couple years later the opportunity to join a community orchestra in my own hometown arose. It was a wonderful and unexpected opportunity to perform again, and I jumped at the chance. It was not a paid position, but my heart and passion were fulfilled through it. Joining this quaint orchestra led me to meet people and gain respect as a bassoonist in my community. I now enjoy the position of a paid private instructor and substitute teacher for the entire music department in our school system. This has brought blessings into my life that I never anticipated! God was faithful to open the doors in His time and this season because I was faithful to honor my commitments and responsibilities.

The way we approach the naturally ordered seasons of our

lives *and* the unexpected ones really does shape the quality of our lives. If we allow God to work His will in us, and trust that He has a purpose for each season, we will grow in character and in His image.

When we trust Him, we will find that He can be the cozy fire warming us from the chill of the winter, holding us close during times of grief or sorrow. He can be the returning hope and new life of the spring season that follows. If we allow Him to maintain control in our lives, He can cause a long summer season of carefree living and fun to be ours and shared with those we love. And when we experience the harvest of our work, we can be thankful that the bounty He gives in the fall seasons of our lives will carry us again through any storm the winter may bring.

Her children rise up and call her blessed;
Her husband also.

—PROVERBS 31:28, NKJV

The Simple Elegance of Excellence

Simple Elegance, The Guest-Ready Home, Time Management

or most women, how you *look* has a lot to do with how you *feel*. When a woman doesn't look successful, put together, confident, and beautiful, she most likely won't feel that way either. The simple plan for excellence will allow you to pursue life's challenges with confidence.

In your pursuit of excellence with simple elegance, it is necessary to establish yourself in these four vital parts of your life: spiritual, emotional, mental, and physical.

When you are living life with a commitment to faith (God first), prayer, a servant's heart of grace and forgiveness for family and community, and have learned to operate with the tools of courage, passion, and discipline; it should overflow and shine outwardly. This is where we learn the importance of physical excellence and how your inside beauty is reflected on the outside with simple elegance. It is so important that we bring the elegance, tenderness, and simplicity of womanhood to our world.

✳ Simple Elegance ✳

A mirror is a household object that gives an honest reflection. Is the mirror in your home revealing an image you are happy with? Is it a true representation of who you really are or want to be? If you could not answer "yes" to those questions, let's set about to change that.

When it comes to our appearance, we do have to work with what God gave us, but He has made each of us wonderfully. The best way to begin improving your reflection is to make a *routine* for yourself that includes attention to each and every part of you, from the top of your head to the bottom your feet. Most Important: Be attractive to yourself first, and then be attractive to your spouse and others.

Start by taking a good evaluation of your physical self. I dare say we can all find areas we can improve upon. It is easy to be critical of oneself.

Then comes the challenge: taking action to improve. I have been so guilty of being physically critical but finding it so difficult to make improvements. However, once I realized the way I feel about myself physically affects the way I feel about my world, I was motivated to take action. When you feel like you look great, you will feel great.

I would like to repeat that our goal is excellence *not* perfection. We want to set a standard that is above average. Perfection is not attained in its fullness here, but will be attained in Heaven.

As I approach this section of the book, I do it with caution. It is not my intention to offend, but to challenge, motivate, and encourage you to capture the best that you can be. It is important to remember that inner beauty is your most important feature. It must be developed, because without it even the prettiest woman can be unattractive.

I feel that we have gotten away from being feminine in the truest sense. This isn't necessarily our fault. Over the past few decades our involvement in the work world has forced us to adjust how we approach our roles and even our femininity. Fortunately we can be successful in life without abandoning the feminine magnetism that our husbands and family are drawn to. It's time for us to recapture that. Remember, *you* offer a woman's special touch to life that only a mom, a daughter, a wife or a sister can give.

As women we have the unique ability to possess elegance—a refined grace. As a young girl in the 60s, there was a woman who I believed possessed ultimate elegance. She was not overdone. Her hair, her wardrobe and how she carried herself were a textbook example of simple elegance. Her name was Jacqueline Kennedy. Because of her cultivated taste and choice of classy, timeless pieces, she could rightly be called one of the most influential women in fashion.

I bet right now you're thinking, "Sure, it was easy for her; she had the right measurements! How could I ever be like that?" Well, if you've ever seen a makeover television show you have probably watched women with a variety of looks and body types transformed. We all have the ability to look our best self. You must believe that God has created beauty in you and take the steps to let all of it shine.

A Simple Plan of Action to Elegance

"Don't you realize that your body is the temple of the Holy Spirit, who lives in you and was given to you by God?" (1 Corinthians 6:19, NLT).

Take care of your body; it's the only one you'll get on this earth! To properly give attention to your physical self, it is important to create a routine of exercise and a menu of healthy foods. Live to the max and feel good while doing it!

A Reference in Faith

Let's look again at Esther to see what Persian law required for their women to be considered attractive physically. Chapter 2, verse 12 says:

> "[Esther] had completed twelve months' preparation, according to the regulations for the women, for thus were the days of their preparation apportioned: six months with perfumes and preparations for beautifying" (NKJV).

Esther's law required 12 months' preparation for a complete makeover and six months with costly oils, and we think we should be gorgeous after a quick shower? No way. Take time for yourself; find value in yourself; be disciplined. You are worth it. (That's right; I just gave you permission with biblical backup to schedule a spa day!)

Continuing on, Esther 2:3 (NIV) says, "And let beauty preparations be given them." Okay, if beauty treatments were important for beautiful women of 465 B.C., then shouldn't they also be for us today? Remember, we are children of the King of kings, so let's represent Him well.

The following poetic piece from the Old Testament (excerpts from Song of Solomon, chapters 4 and 7) is a groom describing his bride:

"Behold you are fair, my love Behold you are fair. You have dove's eyes behind your veil and your hair is like a flock of goats. Your teeth are like a flock of shorn sheep, which have come up from the washing. Your lips are like a strand of scarlet, and your mouth is lovely. Your temples behind your veil are like a piece of pomegranate; your neck is like the tower of David. Your two breasts are like two fawns, twins of a gazelle, which feed among the lilies....

How beautiful are your feet in sandals. The curves of your thighs are like jewels. Your naval is a rounded goblet; your waist is a heap of wheat set about with lilies. Your neck is like an ivory tower, your eyes like the pools of Heshbon. Your nose is like the tower of Lebanon, and your head crowns you like Mount Carmel. The hair of your head is like purple [a head covering of royalty]. Your stature is like a palm tree. The fragrance of your breath like apples, and the roof of your mouth like the best wine" (NKJV).

He gives great detail to every part of her body. He adores her. I believe that in some way, all women want be seen like this in the eyes of their lover. So let's get to work! Let's look in detail at every part of our physical body.

HERE IS A SIMPLE PLAN TO A MAKEOVER
THAT RESULTS IN ELEGANCE.

Health and Fitness

Find an exercise plan geared for women that includes: strength and toning, weight loss management and cardiovascular exercise. Choose a diet that is low in fat and low in sugar. Eat lots of fruits and vegetables and drink eight glasses of water daily. An efficient workout and good food choices are the secret to health and fitness.

Makeup and Hair

Paying a little extra attention to our hair and make up can make a huge difference in our appearance. If you don't know where to start, the best idea is to get some wise (and free!) counsel. Go to the mall; many stores that sell cosmetics will give you a free lesson on makeup application. They will customize the application for your needs, from suggested daily wear to evening wear.

My personal hairdresser believes hairstyle and maintenance of your hairstyle directly affects one's self esteem. Find a stylist that will take a personal interest in you and the way you look. Give attention to your smiling face and the hair that adorns it. It is worth the investment.

Skin Care Products

Use them! Get into a routine of cleansing, toning, and moisturizing, twice a day, morning and night. When your skin looks great, you are always putting your best face forward. Don't forget perfumes, body lotions, toothpaste/whitener, mouthwash, and bubble bath. Cleanliness is next to godliness; I am sure of it!

Intimate Apparel

Building a great outfit starts with the undergarments. Keep them new, pretty, sweet, sexy, and contemporary. Throw away anything that's worn or fits improperly. Buy apparel that celebrates your silhouette!

Accessories

What a fun way to give variety to your wardrobe: belts, scarves, shoes, and purses. Buy inexpensive. Give way to your creativity.

Jewelry

I have my wedding ring and anniversary band and one necklace/bracelet. Believe it or not, I wear only one pair of earrings. Remember, I live by the motto of keeping life simple and buying only what I need.

A Reference in Life

Living with and raising boys taught me to do things quickly. My guys can look like a million bucks in 15 minutes with a quick shower and a shave. But you know as a woman, it's not possible. It takes me about 45 minutes to get ready (of course, I sometimes touch up my hair, or put on my makeup while riding in the car), so by minimizing the extra adornments like jewelry, I reduce the amount of time it takes me to get ready and I can relax when doing so. I avoid adding complications to this process. Do what is best for you, but if your goal is to keep it simple, this is a good plan.

Since I have just one set of jewelry, I chose diamonds and a strand of pearls. They work for casual and formal.

Manicures and Pedicures

If you cannot afford these little salon luxuries on a regular basis, then treat yourself once to see how they are given, learn what spa tools are needed, and then start doing them for yourself. If you can afford to go more regularly, put it on the calendar and make it a routine.

Wardrobe

The first key to creating your personal wardrobe is to buy clothing that suits your figure. To maximize your dollar and project a classic look, buy outfits that are timeless.

In this book we have already talked about the importance of a good foundation. This concept also applies to the building of your wardrobe. For a starting point, begin with basic black. Black is timeless and fits easily into any style of dress. My favorite designer says it this way, "Black—it's the most unforgettable way to say summer," and to that I happily add spring, fall, and winter! "Bold, graceful black."

Here are the five categories of a well-rounded wardrobe:

1. *Formal*: Everyone looks good in an elegant, long black dress.
2. *Semi-formal*: The "little black dress" as the designer would say—"never ordinary, always extraordinary"—is perfect for every occasion: dinner, birthday parties, and even church. You may choose to go short length, to the knee and/or tea length. The tea length pulls double duty because it can be worn for a formal occasion as well.
3. *Business dress*: Choose a suit that includes slacks and a skirt. Buy several tops: blouses, camisoles, sweaters or jackets to wear with them. Your tops create variety. Make sure you choose white or winter white along with colors.
4. *Casual*: Pants, jeans, shorts, skirts, Capri pants, and skorts. Again, variety is integrated with tops.
5. *Sportswear*: Don't forget, you need sportswear—something to work out in and to enjoy your favorite sport or recreational activity. You need only one outfit. Add more when your budget allows for it.

Once you have the *basic black* items covered, add to the wardrobe according to your budget.

A Reference in Life

I have a tendency to buy dresses. I prefer dresses to slacks because I really enjoy feeling "girly" and feminine. Dresses not only offer variety in color and style, but they're also a cost-conscious choice that requires just one article of clothing to be purchased in lieu of a set. Just add a pair of open-toe high heels or sandals for a simple, stress-free outfit that exudes excellence.

It's important to remember that, just like with any improvement we make in life, achieving our best physical self won't happen overnight. We need to make the small changes that lend to the bigger changes. This has been a journey for me too.

A Reference in Life

As a child, I loved the story of the ugly duckling. Something about those pictures, about the story, drew me in. Each time I read it, I would stare at that little duckling on the page and wish I could console him. I wanted to pick him up and love him and tell him that I didn't think he was ugly. But there was a reason I empathized with him so much. Growing up in a family of sisters, I always viewed myself as the "ugly duckling" of the bunch. That is, until my husband encouraged me to go regularly to the salon and spa. In the 70s, not many took advantage of those services—especially poor college students.

The results of the spa treatments were not just pleasing to my husband, but they made an incredible impact on me. The nail polish, facials, massages, new hairstyle, and highlighting/color made me feel like a new woman. I experienced a sense of pride, confidence and entitlement—deserving of the opportunity to be my best self. It was the best gift my husband could have given me. For the first time I felt that God had not given me the "short end of the stick" in the beauty department.

With that experience on that day, I became passionate about tending more closely to the physical aspect of my life.

Start by asking yourself: Who are you physically? Who do you want to realistically become? What matters to you also matters to God. When we're happy with who we are, happy with who God is helping us to become, and we know where we're headed, our newfound pride and confidence is reflected in our smile, our step our practices and even home. When we are our best physical self, we free up our minds and hearts to be more dedicated to God.

✳ The Guest-Ready Home ✳

A Reference in Life

The scene was set: food, live entertainment, candles, flowers, white linens and 250 guests meandering in and around our home. I was accustomed to throwing dinner parties, but this one had required even more attention to detail.

In the midst of the party a dear friend asked, "How do you

do it?" I was somewhat taken aback, but I appreciated the compliment, especially from someone who knew how busy my schedule had been lately.

I stopped to reflect for a moment. "How *did* I do it?" The question wasn't answered right then, but it set in motion the thoughts that eventually led to an answer—and consequently, this book. *Keep life simple.* I realized that over the years I had learned some basic ways to simplify my everyday life and keep my home guest-ready, so that when an opportunity arose, I was ready for it!

"Routine" is (again) the key word. Establishing a routine of maintaining your home is essential in achieving a guest-ready home and part of living in excellence. Keeping one's home is a *huge* task but a very necessary one. A routine that is well-rehearsed within the home is crucial to keeping the stress level low each day. The lower your stress level, the more room you make in your life for God. Excellence needs to be applied to the way you keep your home and the things you own In Christian circles, we sometimes talk about "stewarding the resources that God has given us" as it pertains to money. A good steward is a person who deals wisely with what God has entrusted to them and takes good care to protect it. But the idea of stewardship should be applied to everything that we have—all of our possessions. If we are truly thankful for what God has provided for us, we'll be careful to guard, protect, nurture and tend to it.

A Reference in Life

I learned an excellent lesson about stewardship from being first-time homeowners. We made a practice of taking good care of the house, and when it was time for us to sell it, it had not only acquired great equity, the value more than doubled. No matter if you own or lease, treat the goodness and blessing of material gifts from God excellently. I like to approach housekeeping with three easy steps: first clear the clutter, organize and then maintain.

CLEAR THE CLUTTER!

The simplest and most important act in keeping your house looking tidy is to keep your counters cleared off. Between mail, school papers, business paperwork, magazines, and newspapers, it can pile up quickly. From my experience, every one of those items can be filed, recycled or thrown away. One of our first furniture investments was a roll-top desk. It provided a way to organize an abundance of papers and get them out of sight; the value has been immeasurable.

You can't be expected to give your home a thorough cleaning when you have so much stuff. Get in those drawers and closets, and get rid of it. Clear the clutter. Be organized. *Keep only what you really need.* The rule in our house is: If you haven't worn it or used it in a year, you will never use it! (There are some exceptions, but not many.) Maintaining a home that contains only what is needed gives way to freedom and peace of mind. Remember, if you really have done your job of cleaning and clearing the clutter, the light cleaning required through the rest of the year will be easy.

Storage

We all need a place for storage, whether it's just a closet or a whole room in the basement. Whatever area you have designated for storage, don't let it get out of control. If you feel the organization of your storage area starting to slip, have a garage sale, sell it online or donate it to someone in need.

A Reference in Life

I have a designated garage sale box tucked away that I fill throughout the year. This helps me to clear the clutter on a weekly basis. To reduce the work I would have to do later in the year, I even price each item when I place it in the box. By the time the garage sale comes around, the items are already ready to be displayed.

Of course, there are treasures that can't be given or thrown away. My sons' childhood treasures and pictures are priceless. Technology makes picture storage easy and clutter-free, but memorabilia requires a different approach. For memorabilia, I have chosen to create memory boxes. This is an excellent, meaningful, safe option for keeping precious memories. They are easy to create and still keep spaces organized and accessible.

Once you de-clutter, *organize* so you can find things easily.

Categorization can help in this effort. Here are some suggestions to make your items more accessible and simpler to find.

Kitchen cabinets:
- Each single cabinet should be for one kind of item
- One cabinet: glasses, mugs, and cups
- One cabinet: plates
- One cabinet: bowls and serving bowls
- One cabinet: spices
- One or two cabinets: pots and pans
- One cabinet: plastic ware

Do not put food items and dishes in the same cabinet! Also, keep them neat and clean by not overloading them.

Linen closet:
- Each shelf should hold a different category of items.
- Consider keeping fresh towels on hand in all the bathrooms and the powder room.

A Reference in Life

I used to practice the Martha Stewart approach: buying the towels/linens that match the color scheme of each room. While they looked nice, I was overwhelmed with the many loads of laundry it took to wash them all. My husband suggested using quality, white, hotel-like towels instead. He knew how much I loved the towels at the resorts we would visit.

That was way too simple! Sure, they are more expensive, but they look great, feel great, and last forever, which meant I didn't have to replace them as often. This actually saved me money in the long run. It's easy to keep the white like new, and I can do the laundry in *one* load. To continue this theme of simplicity throughout the house, I purchased white kitchen towels too.

Same with the bed linens: Buy high quality and get only *one* set for each bed. Who needs several sets? They are unnecessary and take up too much closet space.

The resulting benefit: You'll save money, the stress of upkeep, save on closet space and, in turn, make organization much easier.

Laundry and Ironing

Don't let it pile up; get it done weekly, if not daily. Ironing is a means to keeping your clothing crisp and clean. It will also help to keep them looking newer longer. You never want to look like you just rolled out of bed. Dress for yourself; dress for success.

HOUSEKEEPING/MAINTENANCE

I love the look and feel of something new, so I work hard at keeping everything that way. A woman does not live in a house, but a home. Through a simple housekeeping plan, you can accomplish the task of keeping your home elegant, which definitely leads to contentment and fulfillment.

"Spring housekeeping" is cleaning the home from top to bottom and not missing one spot. I keep the tradition of this task, and so should you. Why? When you've really done your job of deep cleaning, the light cleaning required daily and weekly to keep your home looking fresh throughout the rest of the year is simple. There are so many products available now that help make general maintenance easy. Buy the quick wipes for dusting, cleaning bathrooms and mirrors for the times you need quick cleanups. They're great for daily maintenance, but keep in mind that they are not equipped to handle intense cleaning (done during the routine of spring housekeeping).

Traditionally, this intense deep cleaning is done once during the first part of the year. However, I break it up into two parts over the year; I allow myself only one month to finish the task. I spend about 1 or 2 days for each room of the house. For example:

- Spring (usually in March): deep clean the upstairs
- Fall (usually in October): deep clean the downstairs
- Each cleaning includes:
    - Cleaning all woodwork, walls, windows, closets, floors, light fixtures, and cabinets.
    - Cleaning all bathroom and kitchen cabinets inside and out.
    - Cleaning all bedroom dressers and drawers inside and out.
    - Cleaning all sinks, tubs and toilets.

This particular schedule coincides perfectly with our annual summer garage sale. All of my findings that have been cleaned out of closets in the spring can be sold at the summer garage sale. I leave the downstairs for late fall, just in time to have the living area ready for celebrating the Christmas holiday. Any findings in the fall can be donated—an ideal act for the giving season.

Key into simple things that help keep your home clean. When we had a household of young children, we didn't allow them to wear their shoes in the house. It saved an incredible amount of time vacuuming and kept the floors cleaner longer.

Outside maintenance is scheduled during the warmer months, and fortunately the jobs our home requires can be tended to every other year. Schedule accordingly; each year, plan a big job. (Windows and siding are an exception. They have to be cleaned a couple of times during the warmer months, as does power-washing the siding.) You are sure to find similar projects around your house that need more regular attention as well. Look for products that make these tasks easy and simple.

I can't say it enough: Create routine in all areas. The more you can make your duties routine, the more your home will run like a well-oiled machine.

A Reference in Life

A great example of how I use routine on a daily basis is the way in which we operate the dishwasher. We unload it in the morning before work. Throughout the day we load it, and then turn it on before retiring so it runs through the night. Everyone in the household (young and old) can take care of their dirty dishes.

Another practical example of routine is how I wash and make the beds in our home. At the first of every month, I wash all bedding in the house even if it has not been used. (Of course, I will do it more if needed.) I undress the beds and remake them. If you remembered, I do not have extra sheet sets in the closet!

If you believe (like me) that all good things come from God, then daily tasks of maintenance become more than that; they take the form of stewardship for the things He has given us. Even in the caretaking of our homes and the things God has blessed us with, He can be glorified.

❋ Time Management ❋

Time is the most precious commodity we possess. Use it wisely!

A virtuous (morally excellent) woman is disciplined, organized and orderly. A woman of excellence has a prescribed conduct or pattern of behavior that is productive and above reproach. Time management is the key to achieving a life of excellence, and being disciplined is the key to time management.

There are a lot of women who are great "starters," but the true test is in also being a "finisher." Finish all tasks within a pre-established, timed framework. Don't put off today's tasks until tomorrow; finish them today. Set hourly, daily, monthly and yearly goals for yourself. Don't give yourself the liberty to find peace with neglecting to finish a task in the time frame you allotted to accomplish it. Be a hard worker.

Recently, I have set my alarm clock so my day begins at 6:00 a.m. and I retire before 11:00 p.m. Use every minute to accomplish your tasks to the fullest. Make it your purpose to look at your day as one big picture so that you keep all elements of your day in perspective. Learn to write down your schedule. Make this a part of your morning routine. The more detailed you are with your schedule, the better.

If you feel overwhelmed by all of the tasks you have to accomplish, prioritize! Sometimes implementing changes little by little helps to establish them as a recurring routine. Pick one task that makes life complicated and work on that. Once the changes have become routine, pick something else to tackle. If you can begin to make your home life simple, you'll have more energy to deal with the other potentially complicated parts of your life.

A Reference in Life

Now I'm going to give you a crash course in how I schedule my life. If you already have an established way of ordering your tasks that works for you, great! This is just an example you may choose to emulate.

The Notebook and Pencil

Keep a notebook and pencil available at all times. Write down the important things that come to mind throughout the day. This is key to your success!

The Menu

- Mondays: Italian
- Tuesdays: Mexican
- Wednesdays: Soup, salad, and sandwiches (this is especially convenient if you have a midweek service at church)
- Thursdays: Asian
- Friday: Pizza night
- Saturdays: Grill out (steaks, hamburgers, hotdogs, brats, or ribs)
- Sundays: Traditional family meal of roast or turkey

In our household, breakfast and lunch is "on your own"; I just make sure there are healthy options for the family to choose from.

Make serving a nightly meal as easy as possible on yourself. Serve it buffet style. Put everything out on the kitchen counter, island or buffet and let everyone help him or herself.

When it comes to dinner parties, I like to set up everything I can the night before. Keep menus simple. Variety may be the "spice of life" but it certainly isn't always the key to peace of mind. Cooking too much food is unnecessary and time consuming, so keep it simple: 1 appetizer, 1 salad choice, 1 bread choice,

1 entrée, and 1 dessert. I received this recommendation from a dear friend and I am forever grateful for the joy that this advice has brought back to hosting dinner parties.

Your goal should be to make the experience memorable for your dinner guest. Give them the VIP treatment. I like to give special attention to the atmosphere with candles, music, fire in the fireplace, etc. Try to think of sweet little gestures that can add great impact. I often buy nice chocolates to put near the place setting, either by the bread plate or coffee cup. I often choose to eat a small meal before my guests arrive so that I can focus on serving. This even applies to family get-togethers if it's a large group of twenty-five or more. However, when I do this, I make sure to join them for the dessert and coffee so I can sit and enjoy their company.

When I go grocery shopping, I make a list, and you should too. The list ensures that you buy everything needed for your evening meals. Choose healthy and "heart smart." Do not buy items just because they are on sale. Buy only the food items that you will actually eat. Buy what you need. Shopping lists are great for keeping you on task. Lists are not just for grocery shopping. Use lists for shopping for items like household goods, personal needs and clothing. Don't shop without your list and don't deviate from your list.

Dates with Spouse/Family Time

When it comes to creating a daily schedule, your family is to be the number-one priority on your list. Schedule specific times to spend with your family; include dates with your spouse, family vacations and days of rest. As a general rule, we've always planned one family vacation a year, and one day of rest a week. (A note about vacations: We've always committed to making family vacation about spending time with each other 24/7. This is a time that you are able to—*and should*—keep your time flexible so you can love on your family.)

Dating your spouse is a crucial part to keeping a vibrant marriage. It is proven that couples need 'alone time' to be truly engaged in the life of the one they are married to. When our children were little and still needed full time adult supervision; we would drop them off to their grandparents after church on Sunday. Frequently, my husband and I would escape to the shores of Lake Michigan just to get-away from it all. Those hours were treasured with invaluable talks and intense listening. Now that we are empty nesters, we've gone back to the Friday date-night. Choose what's best for you. Just make sure it gets on the schedule.

The weekly family time can be challenging especially when the children have as busy a schedule as do the parents. So I posed the question concerning weekly family time to a dynamic couple in our community who spend countless hours in philanthropy, civic leadership, club sports, humanitarian efforts, demanding jobs and raise two children. Their answer: Time management. This couple never allow themselves to be out of the home in the evenings more than two nights a week. Put limits on the family schedule to insure and to retain a sense of family.

Appointments/Events

No one can remember all those dentist appointments, sports physicals, music recitals, performances, sporting events and games on their own. Write appointments on the calendar or in your blackberry so you can keep them from cluttering up your head!

A colleague of my husband has a great system for keeping track of the family's schedule. Every Sunday he would gather everyone's schedule for the week and detail it into one master schedule. Later that evening, every family member would get a copy of the family schedule. At the top was the date: "Week of September 21st." The schedule informed the members of their family where everyone was going to be every hour of the day for the next seven days. If your family has a hectic schedule, do this and be faithful to it. It works!

Exercise/Recreation

Take time for yourself. Schedule activities of exercise and recreation. The best thing you can do for yourself physically is to create a routine. My suggestion is thirty minutes a day for 4 days and 1 day participation in a recreational sport (like biking or skiing). Do this every week. Set aside the same block of time each day for that physical exercise. Be fit and healthy! You need to be energized to keep up with life and maintain a life of excellence.

A Reference in Life

I was an aerobics instructor in my 20s and 30s; the women would always come to my class with the expectation of creating a body form like someone else they knew or had seen. It is simply not possible. God made us uniquely, not like anyone else. I believe He encourages me to be that unique "me" and God created you uniquely to be just *you*. I encouraged the women to be the "*best you*" they could be. I asked them to remember a time when they thought their adult figure was good, acceptable to their standards *and* in accordance with national health standards for height and bone structure. I encouraged them to think of the times when their clothes felt good. What were your measurements then? What was your weight? Let *that* be your physical goal.

Quiet Time

Schedule your time with God. This is the time to read the Bible and pray. Also, take time to read books that inspire you in your daily walk as a woman of faith. In my experience, morning works best for me; spending time with God and inspiration helps me to start my day out right.

Spa/Salon

As I mentioned earlier, your physical self is important. Once a month, treat yourself to a spa experience and salon necessities. Again, if your budget doesn't allow for it, schedule just one visit to the spa to experience the process and benefits, and then learn how to do it for yourself.

Décor

We discussed the commitment to your home. It is important to make time for your living space. As women, we identify with our home as an extension of ourselves. Your home should express who you are, so make sure that it does represent your most excellent self. When furnishing your home, get some advice from an expert. Most furniture stores have interior designers that love to give great suggestions. Just make sure they know you want elegant, simple, tasteful items that are in your budget. No one needs a sense of "elaborate" in their lives. Less can be best. Being in the position to afford an item doesn't mean you need it. When it comes to material items, think quality, not quantity.

Decorating for the holidays is part of this effort. My advice: Decorate. Especially for Christmas. According to a dear friend and interior designer, the key to decorating for the holidays is keeping in the same color scheme as your other furnishings. Keep it simple by adding holiday sprigs or greenery to your existing décor. Display a few scented candles, and you have brought a holiday spark into your home. Make each holiday a special time for your family. Women, you are the key to holiday happiness!

Our goal should always be to reflect God's goodness and character, whether we are focusing on the presentation of our home, ourselves or making effort to improve our promptness. If our hearts are truly full of gratitude and appreciation for what God has provided, it will be evident in the outflow of our lives. We will always strive to be our very best and treat what He has given us the best we know how.

Take the vision, write it down,
make it plain so that you
can run with it.
—HABAKKUK 2:2

Action Plan
Goal Setting

Living with intentionality and purpose will put you on the path to excellence. Now I realize that hearing someone say, "You need purpose!" can be overwhelming. Because purpose is such a broad and abstract concept, we need to break it down into manageable pieces. We need to figure out how we're going to get from point A to point Excellence. Only then will we be able to realize our aspirations and eventually experience the fulfillment, contentment, and happiness that come from living the life that God intends us to have.

❋ Goal Setting ❋

I think we can all admit that there are areas in our lives that could be considered less than proficient. Many people never make positive steps toward their dreams because they think it's too hard or they simply do not know how to begin!

The first step toward getting your house in order is taking an honest look at your life. Once you have assessed where you are, you can get a vision of where you want your life to go. From that assessment, you can create objectives and ultimately execute the plan that will help you accomplish your goal. Let's begin to pinpoint some areas of vision in your life, write them down and create a precise strategy to help you turn those life long goals into reality.

The purpose of the following worksheet is to provide direction in your life. Whenever you take on a new task, pick up a new hobby, or even dedicate any significant sum of money, you should ask yourself, "Does this help me accomplish one of my objectives or lead me to one of my goals?" You will find decision-making will be more logical and on track with God's plan for your life if you take time to answer this question *before* taking action!

What is a goal? A goal is a measurable, attainable aspiration in a specific period of your life. You should have both short-term and long-term goals (you have the freedom to choose what kind of timeline you want to be on, but normally a short-term goal is from 1 to 5 years and a long-term goal is from 10 to 20 years). When developing your goals, you should also remember to target the four parts of a woman: goals that address spiritual, emotional, mental and physical needs.

Write Down Your Goal(s)/The Bigger Picture

Ask yourself the following questions to determine your goals:

- What do I want to improve about myself, no matter what I may have to sacrifice?
- What do I want to be?
- How do I want my life to look?
- How can I improve myself **physically**?

Remember that goals can be large, overall life changes or even something small. You should have a good mix of both. (Examples: heart health, lowering cholesterol or weight, cardiac goals, improving appearance, learning how to better apply make-up.)

Mentally?

(Examples: become a lifelong learner through career goals, educational goals, determining to become a better parent, committing to set aside time to read more.)

Emotionally?

(Examples: dealing with issues of hurt or unforgiveness, consciously aiming to worry less by intentionally casting your cares on the Lord.)

Spiritually?

(Examples: to know God more intimately, to become more active in your local church.)

Assess Yourself

Honestly determine where your current status is in relation to your goal. If you are way off, be willing to acknowledge the behavior that got you to this place, and note the changes you need to make to get on course. Understanding where you are (and how you got there) helps to give you a clearer picture of where you want to be. (If it's difficult to honestly self-assess, be willing to get counsel from others, no matter how humbling it may be.)

Determine Objectives

List (in simple terms) what you will have to do to reach your goal. Create an exact detailed strategy! Be realistic. Know what can be accomplished in 1–5 years and/or 10–20 years.

If your goal is something that will take five years to accomplish, or even if it's a small life change that you can make right away, write it down! Some will be short-term and some longer. For instance, in the category of mental improvement we listed "determining to become a better parent." Specific objectives for this goal may include: attend one seminar on child rearing, read five books about parenting this year, counsel with wiser people whose children are grown.

Execute

Once you have determined that your vision and goals are worth any sacrifice they may cost you to accomplish, and you have scripted a route to reach them, it's time to put them into action.

Approach your goals with the attitude that they must be accomplished in order to improve yourself and get closer to God. Many women need an accountability partner to keep them on track. If you don't have one, find one! When you are happily reaching those goals, you will be thankful they asked you the tough questions along the way. Have confidence in your ability to reach the goal; as you begin to experience success, you will gain even more confidence.

Remember that God has given you the ability to accomplish your goals; you just have to believe that you can learn and do it. Devote undivided and intensified attention to the objectives that directly serve your goal. Get passionate about them! Effective effort really counts!

Use the charts on the next pages to set your own goals!

SHORT TERM GOALS
1 to 5 Years

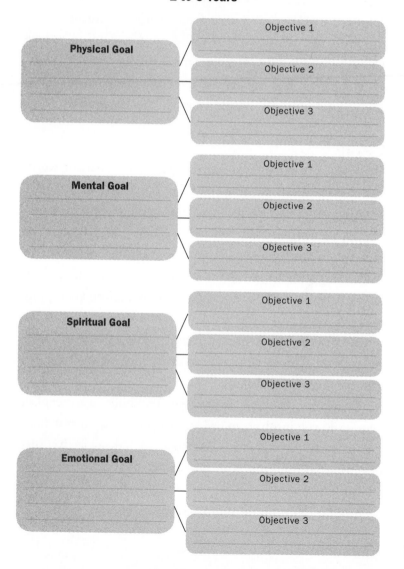

Physical Goal

Objective 1

Objective 2

Objective 3

Mental Goal

Objective 1

Objective 2

Objective 3

Spiritual Goal

Objective 1

Objective 2

Objective 3

Emotional Goal

Objective 1

Objective 2

Objective 3

LONG TERM GOALS
10 to 20 Years

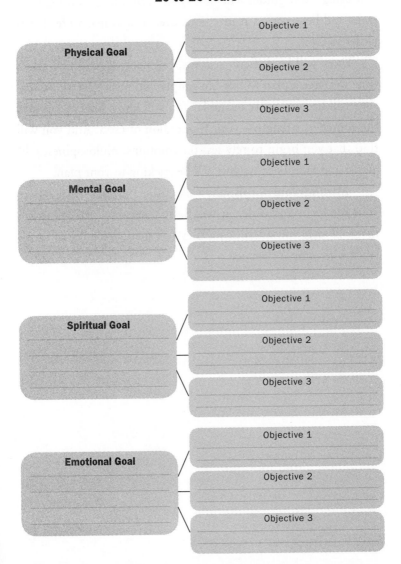

We live in an imperfect world; often times life here isn't fair. But using these guides will assist you in fulfilling your expectations and help you to realize your dreams and live a life that is closer to God.

There will be difficult seasons, but because you have taken time to make a plan to live life simply and positively, those seasons will become more bearable. You will know how to tap into the source of strength—your foundation of God. And you will find that you begin to rely less on emotions, philosophies, religions, and fads, because you will be sticking to your plan.

Making your Christian walk more purpose-driven gives your life focus and order. It will be this personal plan of action that will start you on your journey to experience a life of excellence with simple elegance.

God did not give us a spirit of timidity,
but a spirit of power,
of love and of self discipline.
—2 TIMOTHY I:7, NIV

My Commitment

Don't let our imperfect, unpredictable world or seasons of difficulty and turmoil steal your opportunity to embrace this new way of life.

Romans 14:12 says, "So then, each of us will give an account of himself to God" (NIV).

In just one short sentence, the author of Romans summed up what we need to remember about accountability: *We* are responsible for our own actions. We'll answer for whether or not we truly committed to the things we knew God was calling us to.

I have become increasingly more aware that commitment is easy to talk about, but challenging to put into action. It takes an incredible amount of courage and discipline to stay on course, especially when that path becomes lonely and it appears you're the only one left walking it.

Commitment to excellence means 'no compromise.' It means that you deliberately apply action to what you believe. It is a pledge to do what you set out to do, no matter the sacrifice it requires. It's living with integrity and consistency, and being filled with unconditional love. It is being connected to something bigger than you. It is staying strong in your conviction when it's no longer convenient or easy.

The good news is that commitment to excellence brings heavenly rewards and the promise of many blessings, not only in this world. Bruce Wilkinson's book *A Life God Rewards* goes into detail about why everything you do today matters forever. It is His call on our life that delivers us to purpose and fulfillment. God asks us to live boldly with conviction. For our acts of obedience and commitment to His call, God promises that our reward will be great in heaven. Luke 6:23: "Rejoice in that day and leap for joy, because great is your reward in heaven" (NIV).

Your commitment and love for God must be your motivation to pursue excellence.

I hope that you will agree with me that we must live life with excellence because God has called us to excellence. He wants us to operate in excellence, to *pursue* it. It is my desire that you will take this challenge with me.

A woman read the title of this book, looked at me, and said, "I will never be able to achieve excellence." I replied to her, "In many areas of your life that I have observed, you already are." My sister, we look at the word "excellence" and automatically register it in our brain as "perfection." I explained to her that excellence is not perfection. It is a standard that is above average. It is a state of excelling. It is a valuable quality that we can achieve. The thing that gets in the way of our success is our negligence to renew our mind daily to what we have committed to.

A Reference in Life

Writing this book was an incredible experience for me, but my commitment to the book was tested many times. All throughout this process, the ones I love gently reminded me to remember the reason for the book: You.

I went over this thought in my head: *Remember the purpose of the book: Do what is best for your readers. Be willing to go through anything to bring excellence to the reader. It's not about you, Bonnie. It's about the women reading the book.*

I've learned firsthand that commitment does not come without sacrifice. Even though the sacrifice is great, you must stay committed. Work past the pain so you can experience excellence.

By now you may be thinking that a life of excellence with simple elegance sounds wonderful. But even as you read, you don't believe it is possible for you to ever live it.

It is time for us to face this truth honestly: Unless you are committed to a foundation of God first, and the heart and the ingredients of excellence, this book will be nothing but empty words for you. Excellence will be nothing more than theory. You'll watch others experience this abundance, but you won't experience it.

A Reference in Life

My daughter-in-law is a wonderful example of a woman reaping the rewards of living a life of excellence. Hear the passion and compulsion she has toward living with that standard as she tells her story. Let it inspire you.

> In the rural northwest Florida town of less than 2,000 people that I grew up in, it is extremely rare to find young people aspiring to attend military service academies. More specifically, to find young *women* doing so is simply unheard of. As one can imagine, most people in my small town thought it an extremely radical aspiration for a popular hometown girl, also known as a ballerina, cheerleader, volleyball player, and prom queen, to aspire to attend the United States Air Force Academy. However, God does not discern between majority and minority or ordinary and unusual when He puts a calling in someone's heart, laying out a plan for his or her life. Instead, He only sees a servant in dire need of His direction and guidance.
>
> When I heard God calling me to a military service academy the summer before my first year of high school, I sought it out with courage and passion. Four years after

I first heard His call, I found myself standing in the position that so many warriors had stood in long before me. I was entering my place in the Air Force's "long blue line" on the steps of the United States Air Force Academy. I was over 1,500 miles away from my childhood home of 18 years, knowing no one, fearing everyone and questioning my decision to follow this rigorous path of service.

However, through the many trials and tribulations that the Academy presented during my four-year experience, I persevered and refused mediocrity. As I endured and grew through each experience, any doubt I initially had of His calling faded away, as it became readily apparent that this path was a perfect fit for me. Although being feminine and successful in a male-dominated military environment was challenging, I came to realize that God never promised His calling would be easy or comfortable. Four years later, I was a confident military officer on the stage of my Academy graduation, leaving not only with honors, but also with the promise of marriage from an overwhelming love I would have only discovered there. God's spiritual calling had truly transformed into physical form that day.

Would my life be the same today if I had not answered His call? Absolutely not. Living a life based on faith not only allowed me to hear His call, but also to know that I had to obey it. For me, obedience meant that I had to put my personal wants aside in order to succeed through the most demanding four years of my life. Additionally, obedience meant I had to be passionate and sincere about the path I was following; for those who are faint of heart or satisfied with mediocrity do not survive the experience of a military service academy.

Would my life be the same today if I had given up when His path revealed itself to be difficult and full of adversity? Again, no. A truth I have come to realize is that God does not care who you are, man or woman— or where you are, rural town or urban city—when He puts His call out to you. He expects an answer, followed up with perseverance and courage; for the rewards He has planned for you are unimaginable. My reward was excellence in my life in an abundance of ways—the most notable being an unbreakable character of integrity and a wonderful husband who is the absolute love of my life.

Do you not know that in a race all the runners run,
but only one gets the prize?
Run in such a way as to get the prize.
1 CORINTHIANS 9:24, NIV

May God bless you with his love.

—2 CORINTHIANS 13:13, CEV

Conclusion

To My Readers

My desire is to share a plan that would help you reach a level above average, which I call excellence. It is in that place of excellence I believe you will fulfill God's purpose for you and enjoy life to its fullest. Know that I am cheering you on to this excellence with love. Seek God's best in all things.

In closing, I leave you with this final thought.

Establish a strong foundation, embrace each season, and enjoy the strength and elegance that comes with womanhood. Keep life simple, organized, and uncluttered. Love unconditionally and live to serve others. In doing these things, your rewards and blessings will be many.

❋

We all need support as we pursue excellence.
Find me on **Facebook** under **Bonnie Liabenow**
for encouraging words as you take this journey.

.